WHAT DID YOU SAY?

The Origins of Everyday Idioms and Phrases
Explore the Interesting Histories and Fun Facts Behind the Words We Use

FOOD

RIDDLELAND

Table of Contents

Introduction

Let her rip!

What a weird way to start a book. If you are reading that statement on a literal level, you are likely very confused. What is the person going to rip? These pages? And who is this "her," and why does she get to rip, but nobody else does?

"Let her rip" is an idiom. An idiom is a word or phrase that is usually figurative; in most cases, it is not to be taken literally. The everyday English language has lots of them! Many idioms are so common most speakers do not realize they are even using an idiom. Only when a non-native speaker or child questions what the speaker has said does the person become aware of having spoken an idiom.

This is the second book of a series. The first book of this series covered over 50 common idioms, explaining the meaning and origin of common expressions such as "chicken," "going berserk," and "joshing me." This book picks up where that book left off, explaining the meaning and origin of 50 additional idioms likely to be encountered in everyday speech.

One hundred idioms may sound like a lot, but scholars estimate the English language has 25 million – that's million, and not just one million, but 25 million – idioms. Some of these idioms are seldom used in today's society – for instance, four generations ago, "cutting the apron strings" was a common idiom about becoming independent from one's parents, but the stay-at-home mom wearing an apron has gone the way of the horse-and-buggy, and so has this idiom. Meanwhile, other idioms are primarily used only in very special subsets of society. For instance, people who follow baseball understand that baseball idioms such as "hit a home run" and "knocked it out of the ballpark" mean "to do an excellent job," but people who don't know the sport of baseball would not be inclined to use them.

The idioms covered in this book are likely to be heard on most days by most people. Native English speakers often don't realize why they say what they say; they say it because it conveys the meaning they want to express. This book will explain both the meaning and the history behind the phrase, making this a book that both native and non-native speakers will find very useful and entertaining.

This book can be read chapter by chapter, or it can be read on a case-by-case basis. Most people read it chapter by chapter and then keep it as a reference, referring to it whenever they hear an idiom they do not recognize. An index is included, so finding a specific idiom only takes seconds.

Although many sources explain how a particular idiom came to be, many of these sources are pure opinions and not based on fact. When you refer to this book, you are using a source you can trust, and all the statements in this book are supported by at least two sources. All the direct references can be found in the back in the reference section, and many other books, magazines, and websites were also consulted. Most people don't have time to read hundreds of explanations and conclude how an idiom came to be; therefore, a book like this belongs in your library because it summarizes all these other sources.

Are you ready to be amazed, enhance your vocabulary, and better understand the world around us?

Riddleland Bonus

Join our **Facebook Group** at **Riddleland for Kids**
to get daily jokes and riddles.

https://pixelfy.me/riddlelandbonus

Thank you for buying this book. As a token of our appreciation,
we would like to offer a special bonus—a collection of 50
original jokes, riddles, and funny stories.

Chapter One
A Barrel of Monkeys

Meaning

A lot of fun.

How It Came to Be

Have you been to the zoo lately? If you have, you probably took the time to visit the monkeys, a broad term that covers chimpanzees, spider monkeys, howling monkeys, gorillas, orangutans, baboons, and several other breeds. Some of the afore mentioned are apes. Chimpanzees are apes, gorillas are the largest ape, and orangutans are apes. These fun-loving mammals enjoy mimicking people; if you stick your tongue out, the monkey may stick its tongue back at you. Monkeys enjoy playing and having a good time; you may get to see a game of tag. Monkeys also like to clown around.

Wouldn't you like to have a barrel full of these critters? If you took the lid off the barrel, chaos would erupt. In the 2000s, that sounds like a lot of fun. For us, that sets a high benchmark, and when we declare that something is "more fun than a barrel of monkeys," we mean that it is hilarious. However, in the early 1800s, when the phrase originated, receiving a barrel of monkeys would have been looked upon like receiving a barrel of rats carrying the plague. Whereas we might welcome the chaos they bring, people in the 1800s did not. Therefore, almost anything was more fun than a barrel of monkeys, and the phrase originally meant that the only thing worse than what they experienced would have been a barrel of monkeys. (By the way, if you are worried about how anyone could be so inhumane as to ship a barrel of monkeys, rest assured that they have not. When the expression originated, though, it was meant to suggest animal cruelty, one of the most unfunny things one could witness. When the speaker compared what they had seen to that perceived cruelty, it was to say that what they had seen was barely a notch above that.)

The idiom "It was more fun than a barrel of monkeys" has changed over the years. In its earliest form, the idiom was a "cage of monkeys," not a barrel. It then evolved into a "wagonload of monkeys" before, around 1880, becoming a "barrel of monkeys." Believe it or not, the idiom is still evolving, and instead of "a barrel of monkeys" – which society now interprets as a good thing- the phrase can often be heard as "a barrel of laughs". If someone says you are "a barrel of laughs," it is meant to be a compliment. The 'barrel of laughs' idiom may also date back to slavery times, when slaves were not meant to laugh loudly, they would place a barrel over their heads to dampen the sound of their laughter. This was known as a 'laughing barrel.'

FUN FACTS
chapter 01

- A "barrel of monkeys" is just one of many idioms involving monkeys. Here are six more and their meanings:
  - "Monkey business" means "silliness."
  - A "monkey on my back" means "a persistent problem."
  - "Don't monkey around with me" means "get to the point."
  - "Monkey around with me" means "let loose and get silly."
  - "Monkey see; monkey do" means "to imitate someone."
  - "Monkey suit" means "a fancy suit or tuxedo."
- In 1966, Lakeside Industries created a toy/game called Barrel of Monkeys. The toy consisted of a barrel that contained twelve monkeys. When used as a game, the object was to get all twelve monkeys to interlock into a chain without physically touching them or having any monkeys fall.
- Like humans, monkeys have opposable thumbs.
- Howler monkeys can be heard from a literal mile away.

Chapter Two
Bee's Knees

Meaning

Something wonderful.

How It Came to Be

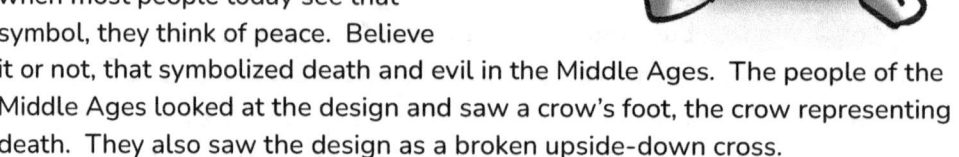

Sometimes symbols and idioms change meaning and come to mean the opposite of what they used to mean. Don't believe that symbols can change? Let me give you an example. Think for a moment about the peace sign, a circle with an inside straight line that forks into three prongs at the bottom of it. Since the 1960s, when most people today see that symbol, they think of peace. Believe it or not, that symbolized death and evil in the Middle Ages. The people of the Middle Ages looked at the design and saw a crow's foot, the crow representing death. They also saw the design as a broken upside-down cross.

Words, too, can take on their opposite meaning. When my granddad was in school, being "bad" meant being naughty, but by the time my dad was in school, "bad" had come to mean "one of the in crowd." It was bad to be labeled "bad" in my grandpa's era of growing up, but it was good to be labeled "bad" in my dad's era.

The idiom "bee's knees" appeared in the early 1800s. It shouldn't surprise you to learn that "bee's knees" meant "trivial," "insignificant," and "worthless" before the 1920s. Knees on bees were perceived as unnecessary. People thought bees flew almost everywhere and didn't need knee joints. Therefore, if something was described as the "bee's knees" before 1920, it was described as worthless.

In the 1920s, though, American culture became caught up in a fad that had recently swept England. Youth would entertain themselves by thinking up the oddest – and therefore the most prized – biological parts of animals – the "cat's whiskers," the "snake's hips," and, of course, "the bee's knees." Most of these humor attempts have long been forgotten, but "bee's knees" has alliteration – notice the long "E" sound in both words – that makes it easy to remember.

Being called the bee's knees in the 1920s was a compliment. It didn't hurt that students were learning about the importance of the bee's knees. You do know the importance of bee's knees, don't you? If not, keep reading. Bees don't have knees, per se. Although bees might not have knees, they have six leg sections, each with a joint. The technical term isn't "knee" like our joint, but the term makes sense. It is because of these joints that the bee can put the nectar/pollen it gathers into the sacs on its legs. The joints, the so-called knees, are essential to a bee.

FUN FACTS

chapter 02

- "Bee's knee" is thought by some to be a corruption of the word "business."
- The "bee's knee" has become the name of a cocktail. The drink contains gin, honey, orange juice, and lemon.
- Bees are insects, and, like all insects, their legs have six sections: the coxa, trochanter, femur, tibia, pretarsus, and tarsus. The joint between the femur and the tibia is the one most like our knee.
- In the 1800s, it was common for older children to ask a naïve child to get some bee's knees from the store; they also asked for left-handed hammers.

Chapter Three
Bite the Bullet

Meaning

To agree to do something that one does not want to do.

How It Came to Be

If enough people believe something, does that make it true?

I would argue that it does not, but enough people believing that what did not happen occurred does explain this idiom's creation and acceptance.

Most of my friends accept that the doctors who treated the wounded during the American Civil War lacked proper medical supplies. Therefore the doctors asked the wounded soldier to "bite the bullet" literally while they mended the hurt limb. The bullet was malleable, and biting down on it kept the wounded from screaming when the wound was being cleaned with antiseptic or being operated on. Although biting on a bullet while undergoing surgery because no painkillers were available did happen at least once during the Civil War – it is documented in the accounts of Harriet Tubman, it was not a common occurrence. Chloroform was invented in 1846 and ether in 1849, and the Civil War didn't start until 1861, so surgeons on both sides should have had access to these painkillers. Between exaggerations told by military veterans and people's imagination, the concept of wounded soldiers biting the bullet was accepted in American minds by the 1930s, when the expression "to bite the bullet" became popular in American society. True or not, when Americans heard the idiom, they took it to mean to do something that one does not want to do but needs doing, and they thought back to a Civil War soldier biting on a bullet while receiving antiseptic.

Although that is how Americans believed "bite the bullet" came to be, the British have other explanations for why the idiom originated and became popular in Great Britain. As you might suspect, just as Americans associate it with American military history, the British associate its rise with British military history. Before the British used the idiom "bite the bullet," the British used the idiom "chew the bullet". "Bite the bullet" may have been a corrupt form of the idiom "chew the bullet." "Chew the bullet" was first printed in 1796 to describe how a soldier would chew on a literal bullet so as not to scream while getting whipped as a punishment for something he had done. Also, biting bullets was an everyday occurrence for the British army in India because that was the only way to remove the paper so the bullet could be loaded into the gun. Many Muslim locals served with the British in the Indian army and found this biting very repulsive because the bullet was greased with pig lard – and the Muslim faith considered pigs very dirty.

Regardless of whether the idiom is based on events that really happened or that people only imagined happened, the idiom itself is firmly entrenched in both American and British societies. We must "bite the bullet" and accept that we may never know the whole truth.

FUN FACTS

chapter 03

- Americans buy more bullets than any other nation's citizens.
- Each year, Americans buy between 10 and 12 billion bullets. Over a third of these bullets are for rifles.
- A bullet shot straight into the air will still have enough force to kill as it falls back to earth.

Chapter Four
Blue Collar

Meaning

Laborer.

How It Came to Be

Quiz time: Why did branches of the British military wear bright red uniforms from the Tudor period until modern times?

You are probably correct if you answered because red and gold were the Tudor colors. Suppose you answered because the red covered any blood stains and kept army morale up. In that case, you agree with historian Julius Ferretus and have heard what has become commonly accepted wisdom. Ferretus's reason makes good sense, but I suspect the army would have put polka-dots on with pride if the Tudor colors had been polka-dotted.

Ferretus's logic explains why soldiers wore red and why miners, auto mechanics, and others who work with their hands often wear blue and grey uniforms. Just as the British military supposedly wore red to cover blood stains, miners and auto mechanics often wore blue and grey uniforms or blue overalls to hide stains associated with their occupations.

Their bosses, meanwhile, often wore white shirts. Crisp, white-collared shirts were expected of office personnel in the 1800s and 1900s. The white shirt was a sign of professionalism, and the term white-collar became a badge of honor.

In the 1920s, these clerical workers began to be known as "white-collar workers" in the works of popular writers such as Upton Sinclair.

Laborers and clerical workers were both needed to create and market products. When the laborers and clerical workers worked together well, they accomplished a lot, and both benefited from the relationship. However, occasionally, one group thought the other benefited at its expense, and labor unrest became common in industrialized countries. Since management was already known as "white-collar workers," people began to refer to laborers as "blue-collar workers."

The 1920s were a time of sexism in the United States, and white and blue-collar jobs were considered men's work. So-called women's work became known as pink-collar professions, including elementary school teachers, bank tellers, librarians, babysitters, daycare workers, and nurses. It wasn't until World War II created a male laborer shortage that women were encouraged to work in the factories or the boardroom. Today, women continue to make inroads into male-dominated professions, and men make inroads into female-dominated ones, and "pink collar" is not used much. The badges of "blue-collar" and "white-collar" are still worn proudly by the men and women in those fields.

FUN FACTS

chapter 04

- Today's blue-collar workers often make more than white-collar workers, but white-collar workers tend to have more social prestige.
- A synonym for "blue collar" is "working class."
- Blue-collar workers are generally paid by the number of hours they put in; white-collar workers generally get paid a set amount each week.

Chapter Five
Bought a Lemon

Meaning

To purchase a product that has a lot of problems.

How It Came to Be

If you have a lemon in your vicinity, pause for a moment, get up, and get it.

Got it? If so, take a huge bite out of it.

How was it?

Okay, that was mean on my part, but this experience will likely enable you to remember this idiom indefinitely.

You had a sour, sour taste when you bit into the lemon. You get a figurative sour taste when you buy something that does not meet your expectations, whether a car, a cell phone, or a toaster. Anything that leaves a sour taste in your mouth may be described as a lemon.

Many states have passed laws protecting the consumer if a product does not do what it should or does not last as expected. These laws are called "lemon laws." Lemon laws require the manufacturer or the distributor to stand behind the product, resulting in the product being replaced, repaired, or refunded.

Lemons representing sour times are found in the idiom, "When life gives you lemons, make lemonade." Elbert Hubbard wrote that in 1915 in honor of a dwarf friend who had lived a great life despite his handicap. The idiom boomed in popularity when Dale Carnegie quoted it in his 1948 motivational book *How to Stop Worrying and Start Living*.

FUN FACTS

chapter 05

- Lemon juice can serve as invisible ink. Write your message in lemon juice, and it cannot be seen. Your message will be seen when the intended recipient rubs over the paper with a flat iron.
- The sour taste of the lemon comes from its citric acid. A lemon can be up to 8% citric acid.
- Lemons have more citric acid than any other fruit.
- Lemons don't just smell good in cleaning solutions; the lemon's acid makes a great cleaning agent for many surfaces.

Chapter Six
Bread and Butter

Meaning

Essential to one's livelihood.

How It Came to Be

"What's for supper?"

Chances are, you have heard that question asked many times. In the Renaissance, in peasant households, though, there wasn't much need to ask it because the answer would always be the same, "Bread and butter."

Bread and butter were all the peasants could afford on many days. On really good days, the menu might include soup as well. Bread and butter were essential for the peasants' existence literally; without it, they would have starved.

If something is essential for one's existence, it is said to be one's "bread and butter," even if it is not literally bread and butter. For instance, if a person gets paid for drawing cartoons, cartoons are that person's "bread and butter." Likewise, musicians paid for playing their instruments consider their musical skills their "bread and butter."

Bread, in many senses, is the secret to civilization as we know it. Early people were hunters and gatherers who wandered where the crops ripened, and wild animals went. When people learned how to make bread from wheat, people were no longer dependent upon wild berries and wild animals. Early bread was butterless; butter was developed when goats and cattle were domesticated. The first bread-making recipes were recorded in Sumeria around 2800 B.C.E., but bread itself may have been around since 8500 B.C.E., long before people learned how to communicate through writing.

Bread is the sustainer of human life. In the Lord's Prayer, Jesus reminded people of that, urging them to pray, "Give us this day our daily bread." Bread was an important part of society then and is still an important part today. All people, no matter their income status, gender, or religion, must eat to stay alive. One's bread and butter, one's life sustenance, may literally be bread and butter, or it may be something like the gift of music that one can use to obtain literal bread and butter.

Bread and butter are not the most exciting foods – that's why Middle Age peasants were glad when they had soup to go along with it, but bread and butter are essential. Bread and butter are the foundation of our sustenance today, just as they were then. In the 1600s, the idiom "bread and butter" was invented to mean the basics of life, and in the 1700s, it expanded to mean the essentials of one's livelihood.

FUN FACTS

chapter 06

- Early butter was simply a thin layer of churned cream.
- Did you know that a law was passed stating that one must have butter on one's bread? Here is how it supposedly came about: When Nicolaus Copernicus, the famous astronomer/scientist most noted for claiming the earth revolved around the sun, became aware of a disease-filled castle in Olsztyn, Poland, in 1571 in which soldiers and civilians were dying, he offered advice about what to do. He noticed that only people who ate bread got sick, but only a small percentage of bread-eaters were getting sick. He concluded servants were dropping the bread and then - not wanting to get in trouble for being sloppy - putting the bread back on the serving cart. Although it would be over 100 years before humans would see bacteria, Copernicus believed they existed, and he believed they were getting on the fallen bread. Copernicus insisted that all bread in the castle be buttered; that way, people could tell which bread to avoid because the butter would smear. He recommended the law, and it passed.
- The idiom "buttered toast lands butter side down" has been proven true in some research studies – and 50-50 in many other studies. It depends on the height the bread falls from, the angle it falls from, and the weight of the butter. Because most people eat two to six feet from the ground and begin with the butter side up, the bread has time to do a half-circle if it is dropped, landing on the butter side.

Chapter Seven
Building Bridges

Meaning

To establish a connection.

How It Came to Be

Bridges are one of the oldest engineering structures of civilization. When primitive people had to cross a ravine, they likely found a long enough log to walk across. Eventually, people developed technology so that the beam rested on supports, and that technology, in turn, developed into the elaborate structures we have today.

Bridges help people connect with an area they would otherwise be unable to contact. Just as literal bridges help people connect with new lands, figurative bridges help people connect with others. A bridge is something that both sides of land have in common, and a figurative bridge is something that two people have in common. For instance, two people may like the same sports team or political party; these commonalities can serve as bridges and connections around which they can build relationships.

In society, people often find differences with others. They note that other people have different skin colors, religions, income statuses, hobbies, and genders. When people do this, it creates a Us versus Them mentality. However, when people look to build a bridge, they find similarities and build friendships off that similarity.

Literal bridge builders have been around since primitive people, but the figurative concept of bridge builders goes back only to around 100 A.D. The idiomatic title of bridge builder was first given to bishops of the early Christian Church; in fact, "bridge builder" comes from the Latin word "pontifex." The bishops were given this title because they built a bridge between God and people.

Of course, if there are people figuratively building bridges, it makes sense that there are people who are figuratively burning bridges as well. The idiom "burning bridges" emerged shortly after "building bridges." Just as people build bridges to form relationships, people burn bridges to put an end to relationships. Overall, people need to treasure their relationships, but once in a while, a relationship is so toxic that one needs to end it. Also, sometimes bridges need to be burned to commit one to a course of action; if the bridge is no longer there, one has no choice but to pursue the new course one has undertaken. "Burning bridges" can be done in seconds; "building bridges" can take months.

FUN FACTS

chapter 07

- Military generals such as Julius Caesar would get their troops over to the other side by bridge or boat and then burn the bridge or boat, making it impossible for the men to retreat.
- The idioms "burning one's boat" and "burn the ships" predate "burning one's bridge;" all mean to take away any means of going back to the way things were in the past.
- Julius Caesar and Rome became powerful because of their bridge-making technology. Caesar once built a bridge over the Rhine in ten days with the aid of 40,000 soldiers and then destroyed it after eighteen days of use.
- Besides "building bridges" and "burning bridges," many other bridge idioms exist. Here are four common ones and their meanings:
- o "A bridge too far" means "a lofty goal one is likely not going to be able to meet."
- o "Bridge the gap" means "to provide a temporary solution."
  o "Water under the bridge" means "what's happened has happened, and we must move on."
- o "We'll cross that bridge when we come to it" means "we'll deal with that issue when it arises."

Chapter Eight
Burn the Midnight Oil

Meaning

To work hard and to work into the night.

How It Came to Be

Great human achievement takes place in one of two ways. In the most familiar way, something startling happens that completely revolutionizes the status quo. In many cases, it is the invention of something new, such as the telephone. In other cases, it is a major war, such as World War II. When these major events happen, the past cannot be returned to.

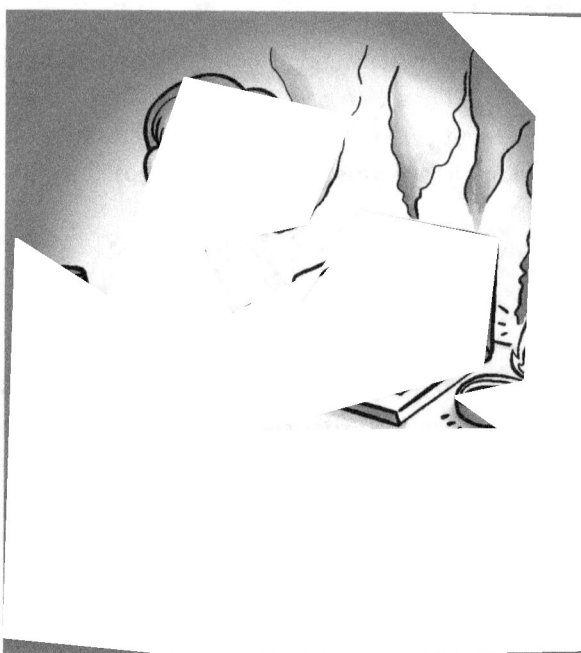

Human achievement also takes place a second way – in increments so tiny that no one realizes that progress is happening. When we go to school every day, we may not feel that we are learning much, but if we look back to what we knew at the beginning and what we know at the end of the year, we can tell we learned a lot. Human achievement is often accomplished in very small increments, and no one at the time notices the change around them.

The oil lamp is an example of human achievement in very small increments. No one person invented the oil lamp; someone invented the kiln; someone learned about clay; someone learned about wicks, and eventually, all these technologies came together to change the world. The oil lamp meant the user was no longer tied to the firepit or the fireplace. Light became portable. People could work at night if they chose.

The first oil lamps were made in the Middle East and Mediterranean about 7,000 years ago. Through commerce, technology spread to other cultures. For over 7,000 years – until the invention of electric lamps in the late 1800s, people relied on the oil lamp to be able to work at night. Burning the midnight oil was something past generations did literally if they had to work at night; today, it is something that we do figuratively if we have to work at night, for we tend to rely on electricity. Today, people still rely on oil lamps when they go camping or when the electricity goes out; also, many people use oil lamps for decorations.

FUN FACTS

chapter 08

- Early oil lamps used lard from animals and food oils, particularly olive oil.
- Whaling oil for lamps was in high demand in the 1700s and 1800s. Whaling oil is not in high demand now because electricity has replaced most lamps, and the existing ones primarily use kerosene.
- Oil lamps are fire hazards. If you light one, keep it where young children and pets cannot knock it over.

Chapter Nine
Carbon Footprint

Meaning

The amount of greenhouse gasses, particularly carbon dioxide that an individual produces is based on what one does and what products one consumes; the bigger one's footprint, the more damage one does to the earth.

How It Came to Be

Have you ever walked along the beach and left footprints in the sand? You could see your footprints as you walked.

Have you ever walked through the forest? If you did, you might not have been aware of it, but you likely left footprints there too.

Have you ever driven a bulldozer through the forest? Probably not, but you can likely imagine doing it. As in the other two scenarios, you are still blazing a trail, but now that trail is doing much more damage to the surroundings.

While you may not be walking through a forest or driving a bulldozer through a forest, you are journeying in life. As you journey, you are impacting the earth. What you do to the earth today influences what future generations of people can do, and even if future generations will exist to inhabit the earth.

The concept of the carbon footprint was first presented in the early 2000s. The concept was a wake-up call for many people who felt powerless to do something about the environmental issues around them; the carbon footprint was proof that everybody could help sustain the earth. By wasting less and by recycling, each person could make a difference. A small difference might not seem like much, but a small difference multiplied by thousands of people means a big difference.

Sounds great. And it is. However, there is more to the story. Believe it or not, it was not an environmentalist who came up with the carbon footprint concept; it was an advertising firm for a big oil company. British Petroleum, BP, was trying to rebrand itself after a major oil spill off the coast of the United States. British Petroleum decided to go by its initials "BP" and rename itself "Beyond Petroleum." By causing the world to focus on what people could do individually, BP took the focus off the disaster it had caused. People began to focus on their footprint and stopped talking about holding corporations – rather than individuals – responsible for global warming and other environmental issues the world faced.

Everybody leaves a footprint on the world, and the world naturally recovers. The tide has washed away those footprints you left at the beach, and the footprints you left in the forest have likely eroded. The idiom "carbon footprint" reminds us to tread gently on the earth.

FUN FACTS

chapter 09

- You can calculate an estimate of your global footprint by going to https://www3.epa.gov/carbon-footprint-calculator/ or https://carbon-calculator.climatehero org/?source=Google Retargeting&msclkid=4f256bfc879416a1d9900 f786432d28c .
- The economy's energy sector contributes 73 percent of the global greenhouse gasses.
- Since the beginning of the Industrial Revolution, the greenhouse gasses in the air have increased by 78%. This is one of the causes of global warming.

Chapter Ten
Common Sense

Meaning

Innate knowledge that helps one to survive and thrive.

How It Came to Be

Let's put five people in a room and then ask their opinion. For instance, we may ask them who is the greatest leader ever. We will likely get five different answers if we ask five people that question. Although the answers will be different, they will have similar things.

You have five voices in your head, one from each of your senses. Your eyes tell your brain one thing; your ears tell it something else. Your senses of smell, taste, and touch are also inputting data. Your brain listens to each of these voices and creates a version of reality. This reality is what they all agree on, common sense. For instance, if you are asked to taste barbequed beef, you will listen to what your sense of taste says. Still, you will also base your decision upon the sense of smell – does it smell delicious? Sense of sight – does it look yummy? Sense of sound – does it have a sizzle? And sense of touch – is it too hot to eat? Each sense was a "wit," a brain, and each rendered a verdict of what to do. These verdicts were then pooled together and united; all five senses gave a direction, a common sense.

In some cases, some of your senses may refuse to cast a vote. For instance, if you hear a loud noise behind you, your senses of sight, smell, taste, and touch may say, "Do what the sense of sound inspires you to do. I've got nothing to add."

When the term "common sense" was invented in ancient Greece, this one sense derived from the input of the five senses is what was referred to.

Over the years, the idiom "common sense" took on a slightly different meaning. People assumed that other people had the five other senses and that, therefore, they should have the same result when their five senses pow-wowed; that is, they should have the same common sense. For instance, anyone who sees a hot stove burner and reaches to touch it should have their five senses tell them it is burning them and to let go – it is common sense not to hold on to a hot stove burner. Common sense came to mean "basic knowledge" that everyone should have.

Needless to say – although it has been said many times, common sense isn't very common. When you think, "No one could be that stupid," you will find someone that is.

FUN FACTS

chapter 10

- The founders of the United States believed in an underlying common knowledge of its citizens. Thomas Paine wrote the pamphlet "Common Sense" in January 1776. Thomas Jefferson began the Declaration of Independence with "We hold these truths to be self-evident," i.e., common sense, on July 4, 1776.
- When their five senses pow-wow together, it often results in people having a "gut decision."
- Which do you rely on when it comes time to make a decision – your brain or your heart? Many people make decisions based on logic and are said to be following their brain, but others tend to rely on emotions; emotional people follow common sense and are "following their heart."

Chapter Eleven
Crunching Numbers

Meaning

To summarize the numerical data.

How It Came to Be

Have you ever wondered why your teeth are not all shaped alike? They have different shapes because they have different purposes. Some teeth are for biting, others for tearing, and others for grinding and crunching.

People have been crunching – crushing their food and turning it into digestible mulch – even before the dawn of civilization. It wasn't until the 1940s that people began to crunch numbers.

Just as people literally crunch food to make it digestible, they figuratively crunch numbers to make them digestible, that is, understandable. No matter where we go, we are surrounded by numbers – test scores, speed limits, sales figures, survey data, and so much more.

Let's ponder a test score. Let's say you got an 80. That is just a number and means nothing. Knowing it was 80 out of 100 instead of 80 out of 1,000 helps us better understand it. The number gives more information if we observe that 80 was the top score and the other students scored much lower. Number crunching is obtaining meaning from numbers.

The idiom "crunching numbers," sometimes called "number crunching," has been popular in accounting, finance, and business circles since the 1980s. The term likely has roots in the computers used in the 1940s, which made a crunching sound as they analyzed punch cards full of numerical data. (In the early days of computing, computers could not store data, so they had to be programmed with punch cards.)

Number crunching can be used by itself to make decisions. Some people use the idiom "numbers don't lie" and rely on number crunching for all their decisions. However, numbers do lie, or at least numbers do mislead. For instance, that student may have earned an 80 on the test, but that student may have test anxiety or a reading disability; a good teacher looks at other things besides just test scores when determining a grade. Learning to make sense of numerical data is an important skill – but good decision-makers are more than just number crunchers.

FUN FACTS

chapter 11

- Humans typically have 32 teeth, but it is possible to have more or less.
- The teeth used for crunching are called "molars" and are located at the back of the mouth. Most adults have 12, three on the top left, three on the top right, three on the bottom left, and three on the bottom right. That number does vary.
- The enamel on human teeth is stronger than some of the body's bones.
- Punch cards are pieces of cardboard with holes punched in exact places to represent data. Each line represented a line of code for the program, and many programs required many punch cards. The largest program (about 5 MB of data) ever written on punch cards took 62,500 punch cards for the U.S. Air Force in the 1950s.
- Before punch cards were used to program computers, punch cards were used as early as 1775 to operate weaving looms.
- Once magnetic media were invented, punch cards became unnecessary.

Chapter Twelve
Dirty Laundry

Meaning

Secrets of which one is ashamed.

How It Came to Be

Have you ever heard the childhood rhyme:

> I see London;
> I see France.
> I see someone's
> Underpants.

Children in the United States have been saying that to each other anytime since the 1700s when they catch a glimpse of someone's undies. (Sometimes, the guilty person's name was inserted into the rhyme instead of using the word "someone's." Although the chant likely began as a girls' jump-rope chant, boys still say it when girls in dresses play in the jungle gym and on the monkey bars in grade school; girls say it when boys bend over to pick a book off the floor. Showing your underwear is taboo, and the poem is designed to embarrass the guilty person to adjust their clothing and cease showing the undies.

Clothing is more than just a garment to keep warm. What one wears often tells a lot about one's character and how one wants to be perceived in public. All clothing is personal, especially undies. Underwear represents our deepest, darkest secrets; therefore, we are taught to respect the other person's privacy through song.

Clothes tell stories. My shirt reveals I had a hotdog with ketchup for lunch; the ketchup stain is there for all to see. The dirt on my friend's clothes proves she was playing in the mud. My clothes pick up cigarette smells when I visit my neighbor's house. Our clothes get dirty through adventures and sometimes contain evidence of things we don't want others to know.

Dirty laundry tends to become a family secret. If someone else washes your clothes for you, they likely know more about your adventures than you think, even if they haven't confronted you. Most people hide their dirty clothes whenever company is coming.

Some garments cannot be washed easily but pick up odors. For instance, if you hang around a fast-food hamburger restaurant, your clothes will absorb that grease smell. To remove the smell, a couple of generations ago, it was common for people to hang the garment on a clothesline and let the wind blow through the fibers. (I still drape mine on the back of a chair and then turn a fan on to blow through it.) This process was called airing one's dirty laundry.

Today "dirty laundry" refers to secrets we don't want the public to know. Therefore, when discussing confidential personal matters in public, someone may caution, "Don't air your dirty laundry in public." Every person and every family has some dirty laundry, things they would prefer the public not to know and, in many cases, not even young family members to know. Can you think of an example from your life?

FUN FACTS

chapter 12

- Lots of idioms focus on clothing. Here is a list of five that are not elaborated on elsewhere in this book:
  - "Keep your shirt on" means "to be patient."
  - "Put a sock in it" means "to stop talking."
  - "Hot under the collar" means "to be nervous."
  - "Has something up his sleeve" means "to have a secret plan."
  - "Walk a mile in my shoes" means "appreciate the circumstances in my life."
- Most people do laundry twice a week.
- It takes 41 gallons of water to wash a typical load of clothes.

Chapter Thirteen
Down to the Wire

Meaning

The result is undecided, and time to clinch a win is running out.

How It Came to Be

Have you ever watched a sports show where the referees looked at instant replay to decide what happened? With today's technology, referees can watch the event in slow motion, in reverse, and see it from various angles. Such technology did not exist in the 1800s, but sports did.

For better or for worse, many people bet on sports outcomes. In many cases, betting is an outgrowth of pride in one's local entry. Betting is nothing new. Cave people probably bet when their clan leaders wrestled. Certainly, people bet on horses they raced in the 1800s. Because a lot of money was at stake, it was important to identify who won clearly.

Instant replay did not exist in the 1800s, so the judge had to be able to see the finish accurately. The judge often sat above the crowd in a skybox and used binoculars; the announcer who called the race was in the booth with him. To aid the judge and announcer in seeing the finish line, a wire was stretched across the finish line from end to end at the height of the horses for the horses to break, and a second wire was placed several feet above the heads of the jockeys for the judge to use as a reference point.

A race that went "down to the wire" was not decided until one of the horses literally touched the wire milliseconds before the other. In close races, a horse won "by a nose" literally; a fraction of a nose might have separated first from second place. Today, the idiom "by a nose" means "barely."

Whenever time is running out to achieve a goal, it is "down to the wire;" the goal may be successful or not, but the moment of judgment is rapidly approaching. If someone "works down to the wire," that person is busy on the project until the last possible second. Meanwhile, if a person waits until things get "down to the wire." one procrastinates until nearly the deadline and then tries to finish the project before the deadline passes.

FUN FACTS

chapter 13

- The idiom "photo finish" also comes from horse racing. Before instant replay, but after cameras were developed, photographers would click a picture of the two horses crossing the finish line because the naked eye could not see the difference.
- Have you ever noticed that a horse racetrack has poles of varying colors? The poles are located 1/16 of a mile apart and are used to measure distance. The black pole is 1/16 of a mile, the green pole is 1/8 of a mile, and the red pole is a ¼ mile.
- The idiom "down to the wire" was likely not invented in the United States. However, Americans started to use it as soon as it originated; it is likely an Australian import.

Chapter Fourteen
Ear Candy

Meaning

To sound pretty but have little meaning.

How It Came to Be

People have always had a fondness for sweets. Cave people had treats covered in honey; they also had access to figs, nuts, and spices, which could be assembled into various tasty treats. The word "candy" appeared in English around 1500 and referred to applying sugar to fruits, such as candied apples. The candy bar was invented in 1847 when the Englishman Joseph Frye took a paste of cacao butter, cocoa powder, and sugar and placed it into a mold. Today, candy is strategically placed in stores for impulse buying; people still love candy!

People, particularly dieticians and dentists, will caution not to eat too much candy, though. Dentists claim candy is bad for one's teeth because it contains a lot of sugar; it will cause one's teeth to rot. Meanwhile, dieticians note that candy has no long-term nutritional value; it has a lot of empty calories. However, if you brush your teeth well and if you are not eating candy as a source of calories, candy can be enjoyed with a clean conscience.

Candy has become a metaphor for anything sweet and pleasing but with little substance. When pop music in the United States began turning out songs that could rise fast in the music charts but never be heard of again, the industry was said to be producing "ear candy;" it sounded good at the moment but had no lasting value. In 1977, Helen Reddy cemented the term in pop culture by naming her album *Ear Candy*.

"Ear candy" may be a term of mockery by the artistic elite, but "ear candy" is highly sought after by businesses in the United States. Grocery stores, cafes, and retail shops want soothing music in the background, music that will not necessarily be remembered but will be enjoyed while it is being played.

Once "ear candy" was a popular idiom in American and British cultures, other "candy" idioms followed. In the 1980s, the idiom "eye candy" emerged. "Eye candy" can mean anything pleasing to the eye, but, in most cases, it also means "lacking in real substance." To be told that one is "eye candy" is saying that one is very attractive, but it can also be taken as an insult because it implies that one lacks substance besides one's looks.

"Eye candy" could be anything from a book cover to a person. In the 1990s, the term "arm candy" came into existence and was typically applied to a person. Whereas "eye candy" could be used to describe people in a wide variety of circumstances, "arm candy" applied to a person, usually a person who was being escorted by someone else. In most cases, it was a man escorting a younger woman; the younger woman hanging on, the older man's arm was admired by all the men who saw her. Although complimenting the woman for her good looks, calling her "arm candy" implied she had little else to offer the relationship.

FUN FACTS

chapter 14

- Although "arm candy" originated in the 1990s, the first person to be called "arm candy" was 1950s movie superstar Marilyn Monroe.
- The first use of "eye candy" referenced the television sitcom *Three's Company*, implying the show was fun to watch but offered little to the culture long-term.
- What most people in the United States call "candy," most other English speakers call "sweets." Hence, the idiom "sweet nothing" and "ear candy" have the same meaning, to be very pleasing but to have no substance.

Chapter Fifteen
(Having) Eyes in the Back of One's Head

Meaning

To be very perceptive.

How It Came to Be

Take a minute, stand up, keep your head straight ahead, and close your right eye. Now, look as far to the left as possible; you can probably see over your left shoulder. Now, look as far as you can to the right. Next, close your left eye, and repeat the exercise, looking first as far left and then as far right as possible.

You likely noticed that your left eye could see a little more to the left than your right eye, and, in turn, your right eye could see a little further to the right. Each eye sees a slightly different picture, but our brain combines the two pictures into one so that it appears to our conscious mind that there is only one image.

A complete circle is 360 degrees; if you were to look straight ahead with both eyes open, you would see 100 degrees. Meanwhile, if we turn our head while standing in one spot, we can see 170 degrees.

With eyes in the back of our head, we could see 170 degrees from the back and the front; 340 degrees is just shy of 360, so we could see almost everything around us. When we say that someone has eyes in the back of their head, we refer to how they have a sense of perception that most people lack. It may not be through literal eyes, but these people know their surroundings.

The idiom has existed for centuries; Roman playwrights used it in their plays. It can be applied to anyone but is most frequently applied to women. Women, it seems, have eyes in the back of their heads; they are very perceptive. Researchers call this women's intuition and have concluded that women have a greater sense of perception than men. They attribute this difference to women being able to read faces and body language better than men and assure us that women do not have literal eyes in the back of their heads.

FUN FACTS

chapter 15

- Having 20/20 vision does not mean that you have perfect vision; it merely means that you can read an eye chart that is 20 feet away.
- A retina scan is more secure than a fingerprint scan; a fingerprint scan has 40 unique traits, but a retina has 256 unique traits.
- During the last minute, your eyes likely blinked 15-20 times.
- The average human grows 98 feet of eyelash over a lifetime; the typical eyelash lasts five months.
- Many animals can see much wider angles than we can; the chameleon has two independent eyes and can see virtually 360 degrees.
- Hawks, owls, and eagles can turn their heads and see 360 degrees. (Speaking of eagles, they can see eight times farther than humans. The idiom "eagle eye" references this fact, so if someone says that you have an eagle eye, it means that you can see great detail a great distance away.)

Chapter Sixteen
Five-Second Rule

Meaning

It is okay to eat food that has fallen to the floor.

How It Came to Be

The world is full of laws that human beings enacted, such as the rule that cars should only drive 55 miles per hour on a particular road, and laws that are enacted by the universe, such as the law of gravity. The Five Second Rule is a result of both.

The Five-Second Rule – sometimes known as the Twenty-Second Rule in more liberal places and as the Three-Second Rule in more conservative places – claims that although food dropped onto the floor should not normally be eaten, there is a grace period in which it can. That grace period is specified by the number of seconds in the rule's name.

The rule has its roots in the laws of the universe. Even early people realized the cause and effect of food landing on the ground. From primitive people until the 1800s, most believed that wiping off the dirt or running the food under water was enough not to contaminate themselves. In the 1800s, when microscopes were developed, people realized that it wasn't just dirt that got picked up by dropped food; it was bacteria and germs as well. To be healthy, one wanted to avoid any foods in which bacteria had gotten on.

The Five Second Rule is a literal declaration by kings and clan leaders. Genghis Khan is credited as the first government official to enact such a rule. Genghis

Khan had a rule at his banquets that any food that fell on the floor was good to eat until Genghis Khan declared that it was not. Once he said it was unsafe, one was not to touch it. Today, most of us have friends who are miniature Genghis Khan's, using their judgment to declare fallen food unsafe or safe for those around them. They will call "Five Second Rule" when something very tasty hits the floor, and rush to pick it up.

Science has determined that the five-second rule is too generous in some cases; it depends on the type of food and the type of surface the food lands on. Juicy foods like watermelon absorb bacteria quickly, while solid food like gummy bears do not. Meanwhile, a rusty iron floor will transfer bacteria much faster than a shag carpet in which only a few threads touch the food item. In general, it is best not to eat anything that falls on the floor, regardless of the time it is there, the type of food item, or the type of floor surface.

FUN FACTS

chapter 16

- The longer a food item remains on the ground where it fell, the more contaminated the food item becomes.
- Researchers have found other variables, besides the type of food and surface, that impact whether the Five Second Rule is valid. These variables, which are not as significant but are still worth mentioning, include the angle the food falls on the floor and how moist and humid the environment is.
- Although the concept that it is okay to eat food that has fallen on the floor if picked up quickly has been around for centuries, the first time the term "Five Second Rule" appeared in print occurred in 1995.

Chapter Seventeen
Flying Under the Radar

Meaning

To go unnoticed.

How It Came to Be

Have you ever shouted into a canyon and heard an echo a few seconds later? If so, then you have an idea of how radar works.

Radar is an acronym but has become a word through everyday usage. RADAR stands for Radio Detection and Ranging. Radar consists of radio waves sent out and listening for the echoes that bounce back. If an object is close, the radio wave will bounce back quickly; if it is far away, it will take longer. By analyzing how long it takes for the echo to be heard, radar operators can calculate how far away the object the waves are bouncing from is.

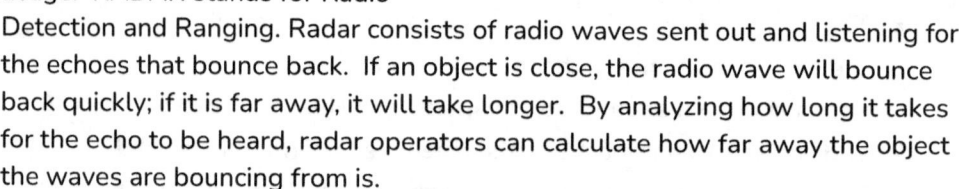

If the radio waves can find them, ships sailing through the vast ocean and airplanes flying high overhead can all be tracked, no matter how foggy or far away. By using radar, objects can be detected and tracked.

Sometimes, we don't want to be detected and tracked by other people. "Out of sight, out of mind" is the motto of many employees in the workforce. They succeed by doing their job well enough to avoid reprimands. While the boss focuses on the lazy or incompetent, the other employees are free to go about their business without the boss giving them much thought. They are staying off the boss's radar.

It is physically possible for objects to fly low enough that they are below the radar horizon. It is dangerous – the airplane is within inches of the earth's terrain, but it can be done. Similarly, staying off the boss's radar in times of crisis or when your teacher is in a bad mood is not easy, but it can be done with skill. Meanwhile, when times are good, you will want to "get on the teacher's radar" to get nominated for special awards, invited to clubs, and get good letters of recommendation.

FUN FACTS

- Radar detects ships and aircraft, tracks wind speed, and measures precipitation.
- Sir Robert Alexander Watson-Watt invented radar in 1935; the British military immediately utilized it.
- On December 7, 1941, U.S. radar operators saw 353 airplanes approaching Pearl Harbor, Hawaii, but the U.S. military decided not to react.

Chapter Eighteen
Food For Thought

Meaning

Something to think about.

How It Came to Be

Food is essential if we are to continue to be living, breathing organisms. The body requires fuel to run, and food is that fuel.

Food can take a wide variety of forms, and different forms have different nutrients to offer the body. For instance, fish are high in proteins, and potatoes are high in carbohydrates. By eating various plants and meats, we can obtain the vitamins and minerals our bodies require.

Most food is not swallowed whole. We have teeth that are specifically designed for grinding food. For it to digest well, most food must be ground finely. (My mom always told me to chew my food 40 times; your parents likely said something similar.)

Meanwhile, if we are to thrive, not just survive, we must also think. Although some people are prone to drift aimlessly or to let the media dictate what to think, responsible citizens think for themselves. Just as the physical body is nourished by the plants and animals it ingests, the mind is nourished by the information it ingests. Just as the physical body can be harmed – poisoned – but by ingesting the wrong things, so can the mind. Just as the physical body must grind one's food but be careful not to grind bones and large seeds, the information the mind receives must be pondered before acceptance.

Just as there is junk food, there is also fake news; these items pass themselves off as necessary but are not. Food for thought – food intended for thought – is the real thing. Still, one does not swallow it without first breaking it down. One needs to check it for bias, do a fact check, ask questions, and see if other people also accept this piece as quality thinking. When people are given "food for thought," they are often told they are being given "something you can sink your teeth into" and "something to chew on;" it is not physical food, but it is designed to be ingested. Of course, as with physical food, you can only ingest so much at a time, so you must be careful not to "bite off more than you can chew" to seek to understand too much information in too short of a time.

When people say something is "food for thought," they encourage the listener to make the thought a part of themselves. They encourage the other person to at least consider what they have said, to mull it over just as they mull and grind physical food, and, ultimately, improve the mind's health by accepting it. This book is intended as food for thought and designed to nurture your mind.

FUN FACTS   chapter 18

- Ultra-processed foods –heavy in salt, sugar, and preservatives – are less healthy than fresh foods.
- Although different people have different hydration requirements, the traditional eight eight-ounce glasses of water daily is a good goal.
- According to Healthline, women need around 2,000 calories daily, and men need 2,500 to maintain weight. To lose a pound a week, women need 1,500 calories daily, and men need 2,000.

Chapter Nineteen
Going to the Dogs

Meaning

Deteriorating rapidly.

How It Came to Be

Do you have pets? If so, what do you feed them?

I have two dogs, a Chihuahua named "Caesar" and a Pomeranian named "Elsa." I like my dogs very much but I feed them dog food and table scraps.

Pets rarely eat as well as their masters. If I had a $55 steak, you could rest assured that I would eat it, not give it to the dogs. I would consider giving it to the dogs if there was some gristle on that steak. Anything going to the dogs is second-rate.

It is not just second-rate food that goes to my dogs, either. If my socks have a hole in them, I will likely give them to my dogs – but I will not give them my most expensive socks that are in pristine condition. One day when my pristine socks wear out, they will go to the dogs; if I give something to them, it is second rate.

In my household, it is not worth human consumption if something goes to the dogs. I am not alone in doing this. Before the Industrial Revolution, the family farm provided a meager income for many people but was the only income many families had. Dogs were an important part of the farm, doing everything from pulling carts to guarding property to herding animals, but dog food was not an option for many farmers. Therefore, all food unfit for human consumption was passed down to the dogs. Anything going to the dogs was second rate even if at one time it had been first rate; therefore, anything that used to be first rate that no longer was first-rate was said to have "gone to the dogs," even if it was not going to dogs in the literal sense. The idiom popped up in the 1700s.

"Going to the dogs" is not the only idiom describing dogs as second-class citizens. If you are "as sick as a dog," you are extremely ill; if you "live a dog's life, " you are living a boring, miserable, and unpleasant life. These statements were made considering wild dogs that roamed the inner city's alleys and the countryside fields, not domesticated pets like Caesar and Elsa.

FUN FACTS

chapter 19

- Just as many people race horses, other people race greyhounds. If you overhear a greyhound race fan saying, "I'm going to the dogs," the literal meaning of going to the racetrack is most likely the correct interpretation of what the speaker intends rather than the figurative meaning of feeling poorly.
- Dogs like to curl up in a ball to sleep; in the wild, this protects their vital organs from predators.
- Most dogs can eat human food – but not all human food. Before giving your dog human food, make sure it is something that your dog can consume. For instance, your dog should not eat chocolate.

Chapter Twenty
Got Your Six

Meaning

To protect someone vulnerable.

How It Came to Be

To best understand how this idiom came to be, find a non-digital clock with numbers that is hanging on a wall. Stand facing it, holding your arms as far out from your body as possible. Stare at it for a minute or two. Notice how your body lines up with the clock; your head is at 12, your right arm is at 3, and your left is at 9. Based on this, if I were to tell you that there was a tree at three o'clock, you would know that the tree was on your right side.

Pilots, the police, and the military use this clock-based code. These are the professions from where "Got your six" originated. Since the twelve lines up with your head, referring to the back as "the six" made sense. Any time you turn your back on somebody, you are putting yourself in danger. We humans can see to protect our front, right, and left, but we cannot see behind us. We need someone there to protect us.

The idiom likely originated in World War I. Although it was possible to shoot an enemy plane from the side or fly overhead and shoot down at it, the enemy plane was the most vulnerable from behind. If a pilot came up behind an enemy plane, the pilot could fire shot after shot without receiving any gunfire in exchange. Planes soon began to fly in squadrons so enemy planes could not sneak up behind them in a one-on-one confrontation. The pilot who protected the pilot ahead of him had that pilot's "six."

Numerous variations of the idiom exist, and they have slightly different meanings:
- "I got your six" means "I have your back."
- "Watch your six" means "Keep your guard up."
- "Check your six" means "Look behind you constantly."
- "Take care of your own six" means "Don't just worry about me; focus on your back too."

When someone "has your six," you can trust them to protect you, just as soldiers know they can rely upon each other. Life is full of difficult moments, and we all need people who "have our six."

FUN FACTS
chapter 20

- The term "clock" was first applied to time-keeping machines that made noises to mark the hour; a time-keeping machine that did not make noise was known as a "timepiece."
- The clock is one of the first human inventions; it provided a way to divide natural units, such as day and night, into smaller units.
- When you add the numbers that can be divided into six (that is, one, two, and three), you get six.
- In Judeo-Christian symbolism, six is considered an evil number because it falls between the number of perfection (five) and the number of Heaven (three) and Earth (four) united (seven); since six hangs out with good numbers one would expect it to be good too, and that ability to make evil look good is why it is a bad number. "I've got your six" has nothing to do with morality.

Chapter Twenty-One
The Green-Eyed Monster

Meaning

Jealousy or envy.

How It Came to Be

Have you ever played the game "Statue" with some friends? In that game, one person becomes the statue, one becomes the sculptor, and the other people become the advisers. The sculpture will identify an emotion for the statue to portray, and the advisors will tell the statue what to do. For instance, if I asked for a "happy statue," the advisors might suggest making it smile, look straight ahead, and have one's hands at one's side. The game proves that we know nonverbal signals, even though we may not realize we know them.

The ancient Greeks may not have known as much about psychology or medicine as we do, but they realized that a jealous person often took on a sickly green color in their culture, just as people who blushed took on a red hue. If they saw someone who had a sickly green color to them who was otherwise healthy, they knew the person was likely jealous.

The association of green with jealousy was still relevant when William Shakespeare wrote in England in the 1500s. Shakespeare was brilliant at creating metaphors, and knowing that green referred to jealousy, he used the term "green-eyed monster" in the play *Othello*; the metaphor referred to how jealousy can destroy someone. As with many of Shakespeare's metaphors, the "green-eyed monster" was latched onto by English culture in his day and continues to this day.

The first use of this idiom is in *Othello*, Act 3, Scene 3. Most scholars believe Shakespeare was influenced by the Greek culture's concept of green representing jealousy and a green-eyed cat he had seen recently. The cat was likely toying with a mouse before eating it, and if you read that section of the play, you'll see that the green-eyed monster toys with people before ultimately finishing them. Some of the things the green-eyed monster will do to you on its way to destroying your life are (a) ruin your friendships, (b) warp your mind, (c) consume your thoughts, (d) consume your time, (e) create a negative outlook, and (f) lead you into depression.

To avoid encounters with the green-eyed monster, try the following:
- Remind yourself of all the good things you have; don't dwell on what you don't have.
- Don't compare yourself to other people.
- Understand what you are envious of and why, and then plan to find what you crave.

The green-eyed monster tends to find everyone sooner or later; don't let it sneak up on you.

FUN FACTS

chapter 2/

- "Envy" and "jealousy" are two different things. "Envy" is wishing you had something someone else has. "Jealousy" is resentment towards someone for having what they have. A person can be envious without being jealous.
- Envy is one of the Seven Deadly Sins in Roman Catholicism. The other six deadly sins are pride, greed, gluttony, wrath, sloth, and lust.
- In *The Merchant of Venice*, a play he wrote before writing *Othello*, Shakespeare wrote the words "green-eyed jealousy." Even the best writers, it would appear, recycle material occasionally.

Chapter Twenty-Two
Gym Rat

Meaning

A person who spends a lot of time at the gym.

How It Came to Be

You probably don't want to hear this, but chances are there is a rat – or at least a field mouse - close by you.

Rats enjoy being around humans. We humans throw away our food scraps; the rats help themselves to them. Humans travel by boat to another land; the rats also stow aboard. (You have probably heard the idiom about all the rats leaving the sinking ship.)

Rats often settle into the wharves of the town where the humans land. Wharves have a lot of appeal to rats, containing the remains fishermen have cleaned, remnants of a grain cargo that spilled while loading, plenty of drinking water, and lots of dark places to hide. Rats have become associated with wharves.

It isn't just rats that hang around wharves. Drifters, vagabonds, and tramps also scavenge and live around the wharves. Dock workers referred to these people as "wharf rats," just like they referred to the literal rat by that name.

Since a person who hung out at the wharf was a "wharf rat," it was natural that society began calling other people who hung out at specific locations to be given a similar nickname, with the location being turned into an adjective followed by the word "rat." For instance, youth hanging around the skate park were "skate rats," college students hanging around a fraternity house were "frat rats," and people who spent hours in a laboratory were "lab rats." It was only natural then that in the early 1910s, people who hung around the gymnasium began to be called "gym rats."

Rats traveled from wharf to wharf, community to community. Rats were carriers of the Black Plague. In 1611 when the idiom "rat" was first introduced, being called a "rat" was an insult, for rats were perceived as disgusting. Even today, someone who tattles and snitches is called a "rat."

"Rat" is generally a negative term. However, "gym rat" can be a term of honor or derision. Some people are proud of their dedication to the gym. Other people who are not into fitness as much perceive excessive time at the gym as a waste of time. Even people who use the gym often dislike gym rats because they are in the gym watching them whenever they exercise or even using the equipment they wish to use.

FUN FACTS

chapter 22

- About one-third of the gym members who begin the year will cancel their membership before the end of the year.
- Only 20 percent of people with gym memberships go to the gym regularly.
- To make the gym appealing to prospective members, gyms tend to place the easy machines where passersby can see them; the hard machines are in the back.

Chapter Twenty-Three
Head in the Clouds

Meaning

To daydream or to be out of touch with reality.

How It Came to Be

Have you ever wished you were a giraffe with an incredibly long neck, one that was so long that you could see on top of clouds?

If you have ever flown on a major airline, you have been privileged to see what a giraffe with that long neck would see. Peering out an airplane window on a cloudy day, one can see a cotton candy wonderland; the clouds are so thick it would appear that one could walk on them. On cloudy days, one cannot see the world below; the world above the clouds is the only reality a person with their head in the clouds can see. This cotton candy wonderland is not real, and parachuters will testify that one falls right through the cloud.

To have one's head in the clouds is to daydream about a magical world that does not exist. The person who is "down to earth," another idiom, accepts reality and lives in it. People with their "heads in the clouds" are often optimists who can see beyond the present reality; people who are "down to earth" usually perceive themselves as pragmatic, but optimists sometimes perceive "down to earth" people as pessimists. When the saying originated in the 1600s, having one's head in the clouds meant to daydream, sometimes meant as a compliment and sometimes as an insult.

To have one's head in the clouds has come to have a second meaning as well. Have you ever seen fog? Fog is a low-flying cloud. When you are "in a fog," you cannot see much - if anything - around you. Sometimes the fog is so thick that if you put your hand in front of your face, you cannot see your hand. If your head is in a cloud, you are out of touch with reality.

FUN FACTS

chapter 23

- The average cumulus cloud, the kind of cloud seen on sunny days, weighs more than a million pounds.
- The highest clouds are 60,000 feet in the air.
- Fog is a stratus cloud formed on the earth's surface; fog is usually near a water source.

Chapter Twenty-Four
Hold your Horses

Meaning

Be patient; slow down.

How It Came to Be

Have you ever experienced rush hour in a major city? Not much rushing occurs on many days during that time. Nearly everybody seems to be trying to move from one place to another, and one or two slow drivers, a little construction, or a single accident can bring things to a crawl.

Traffic rushes are older than cars. In the United States in 1825, a brand-new traffic artery opened to the public, the Erie Canal. The Erie Canal connected Albany to Buffalo, the Hudson River to Lake Erie, and it connected the Atlantic Ocean with the Great Lakes. Instead of crossing the steep Appalachian Mountains, one could take the 351-mile journey on the canal. People and goods could now travel faster, more conveniently, and at far less cost.

People and goods would sit on barges on the water while horses walking on dry land pulled them. As you might suspect, people got in each other's way at peak times. The cry "Hold your hosses" could be heard as one impatient person sought to get around somebody else. It was a request – sometimes more of a demand – to have the guide literally stop the horses so the other horse and boat could pass.

Beyond a doubt, "Hold your hosses," the New England way of saying, "Hold your horses," would have been heard along the Erie Canal. Was along the Erie

Canal the first place this was said? No one knows for sure. If it didn't create the phrase, the Erie Canal is at least responsible for rapidly spreading the idiom and acquainting people with both its literal and figurative meaning.

The Erie Canal peaked in 1855 and began a slow decline after that. By 1902, the railroads had become the preferred way of shipping, and, thanks to the opening of major highways for truckers, such as the St. Lawrence Seaway in the 1950s, in 1994, the last regularly scheduled freighter on the Erie Canal ceased operating. Hold your horses; if you think the canal no longer exists, you're wrong. Today, the Erie Canal is used for recreational water activities and as a tourist attraction for history buffs.

FUN FACTS

chapter 24

- Horses have been domesticated for about 6,000 years; that may seem like a long time, but dogs, the first animal to be domesticated, have been human companions for around 14,000 years.
- The first time the phrase "Hold your horses" appeared in print was in *Homer's Iliad*; it was a literal request to contain one's horses.
- Horses can sleep standing up as well as lying down.
- Horses can stand up and run within 30 minutes after birth.

Chapter Twenty-Five
Hotter Than Blue Blazes

Meaning

Extremely hot.

How It Came to Be

Back in elementary school, I had eight basic Crayola colors. My teacher often had the class color pictures from our workbook. She expected us to use green for grass, blue for the sky, brown for tree trunks, and yellow for the sun. (I suspect your teacher did the same.) She would expect us to use orange on those pictures that featured flames from a fire.

But are flames orange? Look carefully at a flame, and you will likely see that the flame is composed of the colors of the rainbow – and those are just the colors we can see. Although the red-yellow-orange piece of the flame is the greatest part, the flame will likely have some blue and violet near the item being consumed.

Flames get their coloring from the burned material and the flame's temperature. Blue flames are common when no carbon is burned; for instance, a gas fire on a stove will have a lot of blue.

As the idiom "hotter than blue blazes" suggests, the heat of the blue blaze is the focus. The temperature of the fire is reflected in the color of the flames that a fire produces. A red flame is approximately 600-800 degrees Celsius; that may sound hot, but it is nothing compared to the blue flame's 1400-1600 degrees Celsius temperature. Red flames melt tin and zinc; blue flames melt iron ore and clay. (The expression "hotter than blue blazes" originated in the early 1800s, before researchers distinguished between the blue and violet colors of the flame. The violet color is the hottest; at over 1650 degrees Celsius, over 3,000 degrees Fahrenheit, it can melt steel.)

If something was hotter than blue blazes, it was extremely hot. The metaphor runs much deeper in meaning than just "extremely hot." Have you ever been told that you can't say a certain word, but you need to say that word to get your point across? These naughty words are called "taboo words." In the early 1800s, one of the taboo words was "hell," yet people wanted to express that the flames were as hot as the flames of hell. Instead of saying, "The weather is as hot as hell" – something that could still get your mouth washed out with soap around some people, the speakers of the early 1800s would say, "The weather is as hot as blue blazes," and that was eventually shortened to "the weather is as hot as blazes." Perhaps it was because the blue-purple of a flame looked ice cold, or perhaps it was because "blue blazes" came to mean "an extreme" or "merciless." Still, eventually the idiom of "it's colder than blue blazes" could also be heard in society, suggesting an extreme cold. If it is colder than blue blazes – and most things literally are, then it was an extreme, numbing, merciless cold.

Although "hot" in "hot as blue blazes" usually refers to physical heat, it can also refer to a popular item. For instance, if people want to read your copy of this book, this book will be "as hot as blue blazes."

FUN FACTS

chapter 25

- The flame's hottest part is where the object being burned has the most contact with oxygen, i.e., you will usually find blue flames near the object being burned and yellow, orange, and red flames farther from the object.
- Just as "it's hotter than blue blazes" is an exaggeration when comparing the current temperature to hell's temperature, so is the expression, "It's hot enough to fry an egg on the sidewalk." Even on the hottest days in the United States, the sidewalk will only get to 63 degrees Celsius (145 degrees Fahrenheit); eggs fry at 70 degrees Celsius (158 degrees Fahrenheit).

Chapter Twenty-Six
Keep Me Posted

Meaning

Keep me informed.

How It Came to Be

When you have a major news flash– your family is going to Paris, that person you have a crush on admired you back, or Bobo, your dog has wandered off – what do you do? Most people today go to social media, announcing it on their websites, sending bulk emails to family and friends, and hosting conference calls.

Have you ever wondered how people kept up to the minute on major events before the cell phone and the computer were invented? Believe it or not, it wasn't that much different. Just as we "post" on social media, people used to post on an individual's door or the bulletin board on the town square. If the status changed, the news bearer walked down later with a new announcement and replaced the old one. Situations changed, and it was important for affected people to be kept up to date; that meant that one had to keep them posted.

I've seen the bulletin-board system at work. When I was at summer camp, the counselors would post news and activities throughout the day for the campers to keep up with. Also, in the local café in my town, there is a community bulletin board where people can try to sell their items, such as drums, advertise for help finding a lost pet, or try to find recommendations for someone to work in their yard.

"Keep me posted" can be used in formal and informal writing. If you are worried about sounding too informal, use the more literal "Keep me updated" or "Keep me informed". Meanwhile, if you think "Keep me posted" sounds too formal, use the idiom "Keep me in the loop;" in the idiom "Keep me in the loop," the loop refers to a circle and everyone inside that circle being informed and everyone outside of the circle not being updated.

FUN FACTS

chapter 26

- One of the most famous posts happened on October 31, 1517, when the Catholic monk Martin Luther posted the 95 theses on the Castle Church door in Wittenburg, Germany, launching the Protestant Reformation.
- English got the word "post" from the Latin word for doorpost, "postis."
- Because military personnel guarded entrances – which, as noted above, were called "postis" in Latin – people still say that a soldier has "left his/her post" if the soldier is not where commanded to be.

Chapter Twenty-Seven
Keeping Up with the Joneses

Meaning

To keep up with the benchmark of the goods and lifestyle one believes is needed to maintain one's social status.

How It Came to Be

Are you popular at school or work?

How do you know? If you are like most people, you made a social comparison. You identified somebody you considered high status and then compared yourself to that person. You may have compared wealth, social status, and/or popularity, and if you were close to or exceeded the benchmark, then you answered, "Yes." Meanwhile, if you felt significantly lower than the person, you likely said, "No." Every person has their own Jones, the person they compare themselves to; your Jones is likely not my Jones. The world is full of Jones, and it's human nature to compare ourselves to other people.

The original Jones that everybody wanted to keep up with was likely the family of Elizabeth Schermerhorn Jones. The Joneses were a rich family from New York who built a 24-room mansion in the Hudson Valley. The Joneses set a standard for all their other neighbors, and to be accepted in society – to get invited to the Joneses' parties – one had to keep up with the Joneses.

In 1913, the idiom "keeping up with the Joneses" became popular in American society when Arthur Momand launched the comic strip "Keep Up with the Joneses," describing one family's numerous attempts to keep up with its neighbors. (The Jones family itself was never featured in the comic.) The comic began in *The New York Globe* but was quickly picked up by newspapers nationwide. Thanks to the comic, the term "Jones" became a metaphor for both "neighbors" and "friends."

Although the comic concluded in 1940, the idiom remains popular. The United States undergoes fads – pop rocks, pet rocks, clackers, Air Jordans, bell bottoms, Pokémon Go, blue hair, tattoos, iPhones – and those who wish to be popular and/or prestigious must participate in the trend – or at least that is what society tells them.

While many people are proud to be "keeping up with the Joneses," others are equally proud of not following the latest social trends. To keep up with the Joneses means extravagant spending and conspicuous consumption, purchasing items needed for status but not necessary for life that one cannot afford without going into debt, and that may even harm the environment. Trendsetters may not have the last name of Jones nowadays, but love them or hate them; celebrities and corporate gurus who tell society what it should think, what movies it should like, and what it should do are an ingrained part of American and European cultural fabric.

FUN FACTS

chapter 27

- Jones is one of the most common last names in the United States.
- Edith Wharton, the first woman to win a Pulitzer Prize in fiction, was a Jones before changing her last name. Her book, the *Age of Innocence*, describes the New York society she witnessed.
- The comic "Keeping Up with the Joneses" was originally going to be called "Keeping Up with the Smiths."

Chapter Twenty-Eight
Let Her Rip

Meaning

Permission to start something and/or to push something or someone to do one's very best.

How It Came to Be

When one of my friends states, "I'm going to let her rip," I know to cover my nose because he will reduce the air quality by releasing gaseous odors through flatulence into it. This idiom, though, had nothing to do with farting when it was created in the 1830s.

In those days, "to rip" was to move fast. When a motorboat goes across a lake quickly and creates waves, we say it creates "ripples." If a motor goes too fast, pieces of the motor may come off; that is, the motor will rip. To make something go at its top speed and to accept the possibility that it may tear itself up can be expressed non-caringly as, "Let her rip."

The idiom "let her rip" is sometimes expressed as "let it rip." The former was the original saying. In the past – and in many foreign languages – society gave objects genders. For instance, the sun, God, and time are considered masculine. You have likely heard of "Mister Sunshine" and "Father Time." Other things, such as nature, one's country, and the Earth, are feminine. You have likely heard of "Mother Nature" and "the motherland." Some objects have been regarded as gender-neutral, such as pencils.

Ships, rockets, trains, and cars are generally referred to with a feminine pronoun. Everything with an engine tends to be a "she." Therefore, if a train conductor wanted to make a train reach its maximum speed, he would tell the engineer, "Let her rip." As the Industrial Revolution gripped America, steamboat captains and railroad conductors were frequently heard to say, "Let her rip."

Hurricanes used to be named for women but are now named with both masculine and feminine names; many items have lost their gender and have just become a simple "it." Therefore, the expression "let it rip" is gradually replacing "let her rip" in our society.

Meanwhile, "let her rip" used to refer to engines; it can be used to request permission for anything. For instance, if one wants to pass gas, one may request permission by saying, "Can I let her rip?" Similarly, if one is going to try a new song with one's band, one may begin by saying, "Let her rip." When you began to read this book, you "let it rip" and tried something new.

FUN FACTS

chapter 28

- When most people hear the word "rip," they think of the tearing of clothing.
- The idiom "let her rip" has nothing to do with the acronym R.I.P., Rest in Peace, although sometimes, when engines are pushed to their maximum, they tear themselves up.
- A parachutist will open the parachute by pulling the ripcord.

Chapter Twenty-Nine
My Cup of Tea

Meaning

Something one enjoys and/or is good at doing.

How It Came to Be

How do you like your tea? Do you want it to be hot or cold? With lemon or without? With sugar or without? If you want sugar, do you want the sugar melted by the hot water while the tea is brewing, or do you want the sugar added after brewing? If you want sugar, do you want a spoonful or a quarter-pitcher? Do you want your tea with cream – and, if so, how many - or without cream? With artificial sweetener? With a special flavoring agent, such as maple? Brewed in the sun or a kettle? There are so many ways to have tea, and the way one person prefers to drink their tea is unique in most cases to nearby tea drinkers. What works for one person does not work for somebody else.

The idiom "my cup of tea" originated in the late 1800s in the United Kingdom. Just as one person may like tea with lemon and someone else may dislike it, one may prefer one's sport of rugby over someone else's sport of football, and so "my cup of tea" began to apply to preferences in general. In the 1920s, the complementary idiom "not my cup of tea" originated to indicate things that one did not like. Today, the idiom "not my cup of tea" is much more popular than "my cup of tea," but you will likely hear both.

Tea is the most consumed beverage in the world after water; therefore, it shouldn't be surprising to find idioms about tea and teacups. Here are some other tea idioms:

"Not for all the tea in China" means "not for all the riches in the world." (Having all the tea in China would be a tea lover's dream.)

"A storm in a teacup" means "a squabble of little consequence to the world as a whole."

"What do the tea leaves say?" means "I don't know." (Some believe how tea leaves arrange themselves can predict one's future. For instance, if the leaves are full and colored in, it typically means that you will become energized.) No pun intended, but is tea reading your cup of tea?

FUN FACTS

chapter 29

- 160 million cups of tea are consumed each day in the United Kingdom.
- Tea has been served for centuries. The first person to document drinking tea was Jan Huygen van Linschoten, a Dutch explorer, who wrote about it in his memoirs in 1598.
- "Tea" was originally known in the United Kingdom as "char" after its Mandarin name "cha."

Chapter Thirty
My Lips Are Sealed

Meaning

I won't tell the secret.

How It Came to Be

Imagine that you received a letter with no envelope and asphalt on the back side, making it hard to open. What would you do? Most people would probably throw it away, believing the sender didn't care enough to put the letter in an envelope and that the person who delivered it had dropped it in fresh tar. Today, such a letter would receive no attention from most people and go directly into the trash.

This would have been a very important letter to the people of ancient Rome. In the days before the invention of envelopes and before the invention of sealing wax, people used bitumen, the ingredient we use in road tar. By folding the letter so that the edges of the paper met in the middle of the backside and a drop of bitumen had been applied where the edges met, no one could read the letter without breaking the bitumen seal; this letter would be very private communication, so as a Roman, you would have valued the letter.

Paper envelopes became common in Europe in the Middle Ages, and sealing wax, the replacement of bitumen as a sealer, was developed in the 1600s. The first paper envelopes were just an extra sheet wrapped around the document; this outer paper was then sealed with wax to keep curious eyes from reading the contents. A king or bishop could press their signet ring with a special design into the hot wax to create an impression on the wax, letting anyone who saw the letter know it was from them. (There was no need to write their return address in the upper left-hand corner of the envelope as we do.) If the seal were broken, the receiver would know someone had tampered with the envelope.

Luckily, our lips are not sealed with wax – hot wax hurts! Our lips, though, are where most people look to find a secret, and if ours are figuratively sealed, we won't be opening them to blab about what we promised we would not tell. The expression originated in the 1700s but remained relatively obscure until the early 1900s when British Prime Minister Stanley Baldwin used it repeatedly when asked about political issues and scandals of his day. The idiom is widely used today; most people know it means "to keep a secret" but have little idea of its origin.

FUN FACTS

chapter 30

- The first envelopes were made around 2000 B.C.E. in China; they were clay pouches used to hide royal secret documents.
- To get the best signet seal possible, the signet and the hot wax should be at the same temperature when they touch the envelope.
- Signet rings originated around 3500 B.C.E. in Mesopotamia and would be worn by tribal chiefs. When the leader made an impression in wet clay and hot wax with the ring, the ring signified a person's signature.
- There is an emoji – those smiley face pictures people place at the end of their sentences on the computer to help clarify the intended meaning - with a zipped mouth and wide-open eyes. When you have asked about something and get this emoji as a reply, it means "my lips are sealed."

Chapter Thirty-One
Nailed It

Meaning

To have done an excellent job.

How It Came to Be

What do you do when you have done a great job and you know it? Do you pump your fist into the air? Do you let your friends run up and pat you on the back? Do you sign your autograph?

In 65 B.C.E., when sculptors had completed a wonderful statue, the sculptures would run their fingers over it. The Roman poet Quintus Horatius Flaccus, better known as Horace, saw the sculptures do this and, referring to the sculptor's fingernails, used the term "nailed it" to mean "completed a masterpiece." A sculptor used literal fingernails, but anyone who did something well could figuratively "nail it." Because of Horace's prestige, this phrase caught on in Roman society.

Horace was the first to use the idiom "nailed it," he used it to mean exactly what we use it to mean. However, as English speakers, we did not get the idiom from Horace. Whereas Horace was referring to marble, our ancestors were referring to wood. Also, instead of referring to fingernails, our ancestors referred to construction nails. Where Horace started with the term "nailed it," we English speakers got there by shortening a much longer idiom, "To hit the nail on the head."

"To hit the nail on the head" was an idiom that first appeared in print in 1559 but was already popular in daily speech. Whether it be boats or houses, English carpenters loved to build, and when they "hit the nail on the head," they drove the nail in straight as it was designed to be driven. Around 1950, the idiom "to hit the nail on the head" morphed into "nailed it." Both of our idioms - "to hit the nail on the head" and "nailed it" - mean exactly what Horace meant when he used the term "nailed it" -"perfection."

FUN FACTS

chapter 3/

- When a 1,200-square-foot home is built, it will be held together by approximately 12,000 nails.
- The nail is the most basic fastener in the world.
- The oldest nails known are bronze nails found in Egypt and used in construction projects around 3400 B.C.E. The hammer goes back much further than the nail. The hammer is approximately 3.3 million years old. Archeologists found this hammer in Kenya, a rock used to shape other rocks into tools and weapons.
- There are more than 29 different types of construction nails.

Chapter Thirty-Two
Okey-Dokey

Meaning

The item being inspected or the idea being discussed meets my standard. The meaning is often expanded to "the item being inspected or the idea being discussed meets my standard, and I will do as you suggest."

How It Came to Be

What was the last thing you did in grade school before turning in your assignments? If you are like me, it was to check to see if your name was on the paper.

That name authorized that paper as your official version. You may have had other drafts, but they did not get your name on them. If it lacked your name, it wasn't up to your standards.

In the early 1800s, a railroad employee, Obadiah Kelly, would inspect boxes. If the boxes passed his inspection, he put his initials on them. If the box was satisfactory, it was O.K. Only O.K – passing – boxes were accepted onto the freight cars. Soon, other people working with him wrote O.K. to mean that something was satisfactory and could be placed on the train.

Numerous packages went through Obadiah's hands. People would see the big "O.K" and ask what it meant, and writing "O.K." to show that something was passable became a fad. Okay" was a bit stuffy for some people, so in informal settings, they began to say, "Okey-dokey." It was rhyming nonsense but had the same meaning as "Okay" and was intended to lighten tense atmospheres.

The use of the word "Okay" was reinforced by different parts of society. The nerds who studied Greek —mostly prospective ministers wanting to read the New Testament in the original manuscript – knew that "Ola Kala" was Greek for "all is well." Also, when Martin Van Buren ran for re-election as U.S. President in the 1840s, he formed the O.K Club; in his case, "O.K." stood for Old Kinderhook, his hometown in New York, but exposed the average person to the word "okay." (People considered Martin Van Buren an okay President – but they didn't re-elect him.

Have you ever joked, "I are smart," knowing that you intentionally made a grammatical error and thereby contradicting your statement? The staff at the *Boston Morning Post* had fun doing something similar on March 29, 1839. They announced that their paper had been carefully proofread and that everything was "all correct," but they spelled "all correct" as "oll korrect." It's unclear if they came up with this on their own or if they had been inspired by a package that had passed through Obadiah's hands, but regardless, "okay" became an informal version of "all correct" and about 100 years later, "okey-dokey" then became an informal version of "okay."

FUN FACTS
chapter 32

- Okey-dokey first appeared in print in 1932.
- Because okey-dokey is a made-up word, no agreed-to spelling has been determined, and even the pronunciation varies. You may come across it as "okay-doke," "okey-dokey," "okee-doke," "okee-dokee," "okey-doke," "okey-dokey," "okie-doke," "okie-dokie," and "okely-dokely." The hyphen in each of these words is grammatically correct; if it has been a while, let me remind you that the grammatical rulebook states that reduplication requires a hyphen – but don't be surprised if you come across spellings without the hyphen.
- Of all the words in all languages, "ok" is likely the most recognized word in the world.

Chapter Thirty-Three
Out the Yin Yang

Meaning

A great overabundance: often more than what one knows what to do with.

How It Came to Be

Have you ever seen a circular pendant with a white apostrophe with a small black circle in it lying beside a black apostrophe with a small white circle in it? If you have, you have seen the Chinese symbol for the yin-yang. The yin is the black side, and the yang is the white. The yin-yang is a Chinese philosophy that explains how the universe operates.

The philosophy states that what seem like opposite and contradictory forces need each. For instance, there must be both males and females to make more people. Likewise, summer is hot, and winter is cold, but the world needs both to survive.

Notice that in the black apostrophe shape, the yang, there is a small dot of white. This is a reminder that nothing is completely pure. For instance, in the winter, there may be warm days, and in the summer, there may be some cool days.

Although yin-yang was originally a way to describe the universe, yin-yang has become synonymous with the universe. Therefore, when we say something is coming out of the yin-yang, we suggest it is out of the universe's bounty.

Although the concepts of yin and yang go back to at least 600 B.C.E. and very likely to around 1300 B.C.E., the saying "out the yin yang" began in American culture in the late 1920s. Although popular in the United States, it has not gained worldwide usage yet. Even in the United States, you will hear varying forms vying to be the official form, particularly "out the yin yang" (which is what we used in this book) and "up the yin yang." They mean the same thing.

Many people may not know that yin-yang refers to the universe, but they use the same idiom because it is easy to remember. Because they don't recognize its Chinese heritage, they will say "ying-yang." The rhyme makes the idiom entertaining, like nonsense phrases such as "ding-a-ling" and "nitwit." These people may not know what yin-yang is, but they know they have plenty of whatever they have and are seeking to describe the abundance they are experiencing.

FUN FACTS chapter 33

- The yin-yang was developed by watching how shadows created by the sun moved around a pole during the daylight hours.
- Chaos will occur if the yin and the yang are out of balance. For instance, if the yin and yang get out of whack in your body, you will feel stressed and perhaps physically sick. Meanwhile, a revolution will occur if they get too unbalanced in society. Yin and yang can also get out of balance in nature with terrible consequences. If there is too much water and not enough sun, there will be floods; if there is too much sun and not enough water, drought will occur.
- Both yin and yang are considered equal. Yang is male, positive, and the sun. Yin is female, negative, and the moon.

Chapter Thirty-Four
Push My Buttons

Meaning

To bring out a strong reaction, usually making someone extremely happy or mad.

How It Came to Be

Before reading this essay, set the book down and go to the light switch. Turn off the light. Wait a few seconds, and then turn it on. Do it again, this time pondering how miraculous it is that we can make the room dark or bright just by moving a lever or pushing a button.

Have you ever stopped to ponder what a miracle this is? Most people have not. People today take the light switch and the electricity that results from moving the switch for granted. Electricity became commonplace in the home in the 1920s, so few have experienced life without it. Although people today take the switch for granted, people in the 1920s did not.

Before electricity, people had to purchase candles or kerosene lamps and have them ready for darkness to fall. The wicks had to be trimmed and then lit. Getting the light source ready could be a tedious project. Then, in the 1920s, along came electricity, and with just a push of a button – faster than one could snap one's fingers, the room was lit.

To push a button quickly became associated with bringing about desired results. If one pushed the electrical button, the lights came on. The idiom "to push one's buttons" also applies to people. Just as if one knew where to push the button on the light switch to get light, a skillful person knew exactly what to say to make another person feel extremely good or angry. A smooth speaker could say just the right words to have someone cater to their every need; likewise, a skillful speaker could turn a well-tempered individual into a raging madman with just a few simple words – such speakers "know what buttons to push."

The idiom suggests that people are just like machines; if you do this, you will get that. This is partially true; the unconscious part of our brain thinks fast, providing an instant reaction. This "fight or flight" response often saves our lives, for we don't have time to understand the situation fully. However, to avoid "having your buttons pushed," "your switch flipped," "your crank turned," or your "trigger tripped," consciously become aware of how you are acting. While someone who "pushes your buttons" may make you lash out, consciously become aware of what you are doing and regain control of yourself. Likewise, if somebody's praise makes you gush with embarrassment, become aware that you are being manipulated and regain control of the situation. People will be able to "push your buttons" less if you understand what your buttons are. Everybody has metaphorical buttons, and other people succeed in pushing them – but ultimately, you can switch them back as they were.

FUN FACTS

chapter 34

- Although pushbuttons are often pictured as flat, if you run your finger over one, you will likely find it is grooved so that your finger sits in the center.
- The push button is an example of people and machines interacting with one another mechanically. Although most people today would not understand, many people of the 1920s were intimidated by having to touch a machine.
- In 1920, about 35% of U.S. homes had electricity; by 1929, 85% of non-rural homes had it.

Chapter Thirty-Five
Queen Bee

Meaning

A woman who has great power.

How It Came to Be

Have you ever been asked, "If you were an animal, what would you be?" It is an innocent-sounding question, but the answer reveals much about your personality. (My answer is a Basset Hound, and when asked the follow-up question why I choose to be a Basset Hound, I reply, "Because I like to hunt [for knowledge], I am loyal, and I like to make people laugh." There is no wrong answer.

Did you, by any chance, say that you wanted to be a queen bee? If so, you likely admire many of the traits of a queen bee. In 1973, psychologists coined the term "Queen Bee Syndrome." They said that a queen bee was a person who treated females worse than she treated men, just as queen bees in the wild do when fending off would-be rival queens. They described a queen bee as a woman in authority. They said that women who succeeded as queen bees were hard on other women because they didn't think it fair that other women had it easy since they had not.

Popular culture latched on to this term. Any woman wielding power over other people – whether through an official office or social status – could be described as a queen bee. The queen bee typically had the men wanting to serve her and the women submitting themselves to her. Just as a queen bee rules in a honey hive, the queen bee in the hive of business and industry has the final say.

Today, sociologists have determined that some women still have a Queen Bee Syndrome, but that, on the whole, the Queen Bee Syndrome is no longer prevalent in society. Women in business and industry now attempt to help each other succeed.

FUN FACTS
chapter 35

- Until the 1700s, when bees began to be studied in detail, people assumed that a king bee oversaw the hive.
- The queen bee will live longer than any other bee in the hive will live; the queen bee will live between two and seven years.
- A queen bee can lay 3,000 eggs per day.
- Queens lay fertilized eggs and unfertilized eggs. Unfertilized eggs become males. Fertilized eggs that are fed royal jelly become queens; the rest of the fertilized eggs become worker bees.
- Queens control the atmosphere of their colony through the scents they release. (Even the animal kingdom understands aromatherapy.)

Chapter Thirty-Six
Red Tape

Meaning

Unnecessary steps that are required to accomplish something

How It Came to Be

How do you keep track of a valuable piece of paper that is important to you? Some people clip it onto a clipboard. Some put it in a folder. Some laminate it. Some put it in a special tray or pigeon-hole slot.

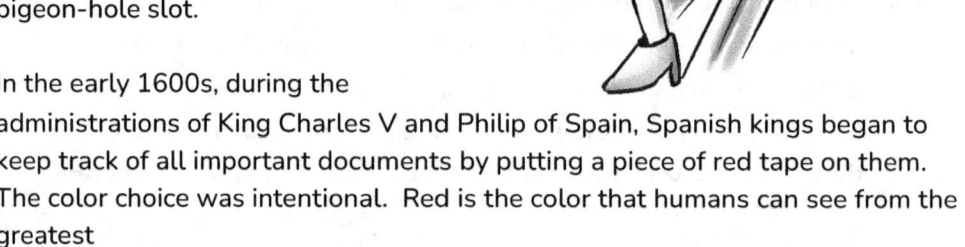

In the early 1600s, during the administrations of King Charles V and Philip of Spain, Spanish kings began to keep track of all important documents by putting a piece of red tape on them. The color choice was intentional. Red is the color that humans can see from the greatest distance; hence, today, stoplights have a red bulb, and ambulances have red lights. The red tape helped the important document to stand out from other documents on their desk.

Other European monarchs, including King Henry the Eighth of England, quickly picked up their business practice of distinguishing important papers from less important papers. When King Henry the Eighth wanted a divorce from his first wife, he sent the divorce document wrapped in a red ribbon to the Pope for approval. Notice that red tape meant a document was extremely important in those days.

Around 1776, the meaning of "red tape" began to change. England still used red tape to signify important documents, but many people in the thirteen American colonies perceived the laws England classified as important and burdensome. The colonies wanted to do away with much of the red tape.

When the colonies grew into the United States, the negative connotation of red tape continued. Today, red tape still applies to tedious or nit-picky laws that must be followed to the letter, but it applies to business and other settings. Many people want to "cut through the red tape" and meet their goal without performing all the tedious steps. Believe it or not, sometimes even politicians and bureaucrats want to make processes simpler; for instance, many Canadian areas have passed the Red Tape Reduction Act, and the European Union sponsors an annual contest to find a way to reduce bureaucratic procedures.

Red tape is not tape; it is a red, woven cotton fabric. Because the red dye sometimes stains the important documents it is wrapped around if it sits on it too long, the U.S. National Archives has pushed the federal government to use white cotton fabric instead of red. Bureaucracy will likely never go away, but the red fabric is becoming a thing of the past.

FUN FACTS

chapter 36

- In many legislative bodies, "red tape" is used today to refer to unnecessary tedious steps, whereas "administrative burden" refers to tedious but necessary steps.
- King Charles V of Spain marked all his important papers with red ribbon; less important files were held together with white string.
- Does the government create a lot of red tape? Consider this: In 1864 the U.S. War Department ordered 158 miles of red tape.

Chapter Thirty-Seven
Reflect on It

Meaning

To ponder something or to recall something from the past with close, particular attention.

How It Came to Be

Look in a mirror and tell me what you see.

Chances are, what you see – no matter what it is – is very close to the image reflected by the mirror. The mirrors we have today usually reflect a very accurate image.

This has not always been the case. The first mirror was invented about 8,000 years ago in Anatolia, a part of modern-day Turkey. Unlike our crystal-clear mirrors, the first mirrors were very foggy and reflected greatly distorted images. (If you think mirrors still can't distort an image, go to the Fun House/The House of Mirrors the next time the carnival is in town.)

Mirrors greatly improved as society improved. In the 1700s, the Venetians learned to coat glass with tin and mercury. By the 1800s, their technique, a secret for years, was known throughout Europe; manufacturers also found a way to replace the toxic mercury with silver nitrate. Today, most mirrors are aluminum.

The idiom "reflect on it" refers to reflecting on something mental – an idea or an experience – instead of something physical, such as how pretty your face is. Although the object in a mirror may look close to the real object, remember that the mirror will never perfectly match the real object. As you ponder the item and think about it, you can get a good idea, but always remember that what your mind conjures is not the perfect image.

To "reflect on something" is an idiom featuring you doing the reflecting. In the idiom "a reflection of," you are being viewed as a mirror image of the other group members. For instance, you may be a reflection of your family, your school, or your community. When people say that you are a "reflection," they mean that you provide a good representation of the group. Of course, no one person will perfectly model a group, so relying on such a reflection can lead to stereotyping.

Even though reflections are imperfect, taking time to reflect upon things is a good habit. By reflecting, one takes control of the circumstances of one's life, and one no longer drifts through life aimlessly. Sample reflection questions you could ask yourself include, "What could I have done better?" and "What did I do well?"

FUN FACTS

chapter 37

- Cultures worldwide invented the mirror independently at different times and with different materials. In modern Turkey, the first mirrors were made of obsidian volcanic lava in about 6,000 B.C.E. The mirrors developed in Egypt and Mesopotamia in 4000 B.C.E. were made of bronze. Mirrors were first invented in South America out of stones around 2000 B.C.E. In India, China, and the Orient, the mirror was developed about 2000 B.C.E. as well, but they were made from bronze and copper.
- In all cultures, the first mirror frames were either wood or wood and gesso, a type of glue.
- In an informal setting, you "reflect on something." In a formal setting, the correct form of the idiom is to "reflect upon something."
- Although you can reflect on the past or an idea suggested in the past, you cannot "reflect" on the present or the future. If you think about the present or the future, you are "contemplating."

Chapter Thirty-Eight
Run it up the Flagpole

Meaning

To offer an idea and then judge the reception to it.

How It Came to Be

After breakfast at summer camp, we had a flag-raising ceremony each morning. Everybody would file out of the cafeteria and trek up the hill to the flagpole. At the pole, we would watch as three camp staff diligently prepared the flag to raise it. The staff member on the end closest to the pole would start to unfold it and then give it to the staff member at the other end; the person in the middle held their arms outstretched under the flag to make sure the flag did not touch the ground. Once the flag was unfolded, the staff member by the pole clipped the flag to the pulley and raised it. Everybody saluted as the flag went up. We would then say the Pledge of Allegiance and sing a patriotic chorus.

One morning we came out to the flagpole and found that the rope's clips were not by the pulley. We looked up and saw Doug's handiwork; he had clipped a bra to the flagpole and raised it. He later claimed to be curious if anybody would salute. (The girl got him back, though; she found his soaking wet swimming suit drying on the clothesline outside his cabin and took it to the Sweet Shop, where she put it in the freezer.)

The idiom "run it up the flagpole" does figuratively what Doug did literally – it takes an idea, puts it out in public for all to see, and then waits to see if anybody shows reverence for it. Although the idiom is often "run it up the flagpole," it is sometimes expanded to be, "Let's run it up the flagpole and see if anybody salutes."

The idiom began on Madison Avenue in the 1950s. Marketers would offer one idea after another to executives; that is, they would run the idea up the flagpole. If the executive liked the idea, the idea was implemented and respected, just like the flag.

FUN FACTS

chapter 38

- The first fabric flags we have today were created over 2,000 years ago, and the flagpole is thought to have been created immediately after the fabric flag.
- Almost all flags are horizontal; vertical exceptions exist in countries with scarce wind.
- The tallest free-standing flagpole in the world is 662.57 feet in Cario, Egypt.
- The idiom "run it up the flagpole" has inspired a holiday in the United States, Run It Up the Flagpole Day. Run It Up the Flagpole Day is celebrated on January 2; it aims to share one's New Year's resolutions and get feedback from friends.

Chapter Thirty-Nine
Sit Tight

Meaning

Be patient; stay where you are; don't physically move or do anything radical.

How It Came to Be

Have you ever played Freeze Tag? It is played just like regular Tag, except when touched by It, you must stand in the exact pose that you were touched. It then continues to attempt to tag all the other participants.

The onlooker will see people standing like statues in various stages of stride and cowering as if they were still trying to avoid its touch. Those tagged sitting on a bench or a chair are perfect examples of someone taking the "sit tight" idiom literally.

Sitting tight likely began as a means of survival. When choosing between "fight or flight," sometimes neither is the best solution, so one will sit tight. For instance, if you encounter a mean Pitbull, you cannot outrun it and can't fight it. Instead, you will "sit tight," freeze, and hope the dog forgets about you. If you run, the dog is going to run after you. If you choose to fight, the dog will attack you. The only way to survive a mean dog is to sit tight, try to convince it that you are not a threat, and hope it loses interest in you. Any sudden movement and you are Pitbull chow.

The concept of sitting tight dates back to our prehistoric ancestors. The idiom itself, though, entered culture through a variety of means. It may have begun in the early 1600s when people would "sit close," drawing their knees up to their chin as they pondered about the world around them. It may also have come from horse training in the 1700s. First-time riders were advised to "sit tight" to avoid being thrown from the horse. By sitting tight, they would eventually acquire the skill of horseback riding. Although different fields used the idiom "sit tight," it meant "to be patient" in all of them.

"Sit tight" has various degrees. Although it always means to be patient, it sometimes means to stay in the vicinity where one is, whereas other times, it means not to move at all. Likewise, in some cases, it means not doing anything radical; in others, it means not taking action. Whenever you are given instructions to sit tight – and everyone from generals to parents use this idiom – be sure to ask for clarification if you doubt what the speaker wants you to do.

FUN FACTS

chapter 39

- Thin people sit 2.5 hours less per day than obese people.
- Researchers have found that having patience reduces depression.
- Researchers also found that when people with patience finally decide, they act quickly. Meanwhile, people who decide quickly are prone to procrastinate.

Chapter Forty
Son of a Gun

Meaning

When used as a noun, it affectionately describes someone who doesn't always do things the way society expects them to be done.

When used as an exclamation, it means surprise or annoyance.

How It Came to Be

Have you ever gotten homesick?

When you are homesick, all you can think about is returning to your family. From children going off to school for the first time to teenagers going to summer camp to adults going on business trips, people of all ages are liable to get homesick.

In the 1700s, the British Navy was having trouble keeping morale high in the navy. Many of the sailors were homesick. They missed their wives and sweethearts. The British Navy had jobs to do to protect the country, so letting the homesick men go home was not an option. However, the Navy did the next best thing. Although the husband might not be able to go home to be with the wife, captains realized that the wives and sweethearts could come and join him on the ship. The Navy had rules that said this could not be done, but captains needed a good crew willing to pretend not to see the women and girlfriends the men brought on board.

The navy trips sometimes lasted months, so, as one might suspect, some children happened to be born on the ships. These proud military men now had offspring, the soldier was a gunner, and the child was a son of a gun. Being a son of a gun for many boys was a grand title. However, many sailors found having infants and toddlers on the boat very annoying and, when catching one in mischief, would sigh exasperatedly, "Son of a gun."

The meaning of the idiom shifted over time. "Son of a gun" eventually meant "the bratty child of a sailor." From there, the term came to mean "any bratty person" and from there to mean "anyone who didn't always do things the way society expected them to be done."

FUN FACTS

chapter 40

- Women on ships gave birth in the area between the broadside guns. This was so that the main aisles, gangways, and crew decks were always accessible.
- The fact that "son" and "gun" rhyme may explain why this idiom is easy to remember.
- If a woman did not know her child's father, in the ship's logs, the name was recorded as "A. Gun."

Chapter Forty-One
Stir the Pot

Meaning

To deliberately agitate a situation.

How It Came to Be

Have you made a stew recently? If you have, you likely added chopped meat, chunks of potatoes, slices of carrots, pieces of celery, and water to a pot and then set the pot on a stove to boil. As the food boiled, you occasionally stirred the pot; you took a wooden spoon and rotated it in the water, making all the ingredients move. Most of the ingredients had likely settled to the bottom, and by stirring, you kept them from burning and sticking to the pan. Also stirring the ingredients also caused them to release flavor into the water, creating a unique taste to complement each of their tastes.

The school or work environment can be considered a pot of stew. In that pot a re housed lots of individuals. When left alone, those individuals may not interact with each other. However, when a pot stirrer is at work, these people are much more likely to interact with each other – and usually not in a good way. Pot stirring is usually a bullying technique, influencing others to pick on a person. Pot stirrers often gossip, tell half-truths, and sometimes outrightly lie to cause their victim to be ostracized. For instance, the pot stirrer may tell someone what another person said about them, getting the other person angry enough to confront the speaker. Pot stirrers like to keep things tense.

Pot stirrers sometimes have better motives than starting arguments to watch people fight. Sometimes, the pot stirrer seeks to make others aware of an injustice being done. Much change needs to happen in society, and pot stirrers are advocates who won't rest until it is achieved. By keeping the pot stirred, justice is eventually dispersed.

Although stew has existed since early human society – scientists say the earliest evidence of stew is found in Japan, possibly as early as 14,000 B.C.E., the idiom "stirring the pot" entered the English language during the 1500s. Most people have seen a pot stirred and witnessed the effects, so the idiom became and has remained a part of culture since. The "stirring the pot" idiom eventually - approximately 400 years later, led to another idiom, "pot stirrer." Be cautious when using these idioms. Because pot stirrers are normally stirring up unnecessary trouble, calling someone "a pot stirrer" or accusing one of "stirring the pot" is generally not something one wants to be associated with.

FUN FACTS

- Before pottery was invented, people stuffed stew ingredients into animal intestines to cook.
- Pottery was invented around 10,000 B.C.E.
- In Amazonian culture, the first soup bowls were turtle shells.
- Because stew simmers in a slow, moist heat for a long time in the cooking process, meat pieces that would otherwise be wasted can be salvaged by using them in a stew. Meats have often been scarce in societies, and therefore stews have been popular in most cultures, past and present, around the world.

Chapter Forty-Two
Stop and Smell the Roses

Meaning

Take time to relax and appreciate what is around you.

How It Came to Be

Have you ever thought about writing your life story? Do you think you would divide your life into episodes? Would you provide facts or tell what happened and analyze why it happened? Would you advise your readers as you bring your book to a close?

Walter, "the Haig" Hagen, known by many as the father of professional golf, wrote his autobiography, The Walter Hagen Story, in the 1960s. Walter chose to end his book with some advice which became paraphrased as "take time to smell the roses."

Today, the average person will not read an autobiography about a golfer...and the same was true in the 1960s. However, golfers would certainly be interested in reading it, and so were the golfers in the 1960s. Golfers, of course, do more than golf; they share their wisdom with the people they come into contact with.

Even with golfers sharing it with their non-golfing friends, the idiom might not have caught on and held on if it hadn't been for one golf-loving doctor, the doctor of music legend Doc Severinsen. When Doc Severinsen, an outstanding trumpet player serving as the conductor of the *Tonight Show* television program, was advised by this golfer to "stop and smell the roses," he fell in love with the line. He and the American singer-songwriter Mac Davis got acquainted one night before the *Tonight Show* got underway; Mac was making a guest appearance. Doc told Mac about the line and his desire to write a song around it. Mac offered to work with him, and together they used the phrase in a hit song about taking time to appreciate what is around oneself, further endearing the idiom into American culture. The song, *Stop and Smell the Roses*, stressed that many people were moving through life from one crisis to another and not taking time to appreciate the people around them or the present moment. The songwriters used the rose as a symbol of beauty and suggested that beauty was all around one if one would take the time to look at it. As most songs in popular culture do, *Stop and Smell the Roses* faded into obscurity, but the idiom was now firmly rooted in American culture. Today, most people have not heard Doc and Mac's song or read Hagen's book, but they have heard the idiom.

FUN FACTS

chapter 42

- A study at Rutgers University determined that stopping to smell the roses is not just an idiom; it is also good advice to be taken literally.
- Mac Davis did most of the writing of "Stop and Smell the Roses." Although one might suspect he was looking at a rose garden when he wrote it, he was not; he was on vacation in Hawaii then.
- The sweet scent of a rose comes from perfume glands on the flower's petals.
- We smell roses – and all smell, for that matter - because chemical molecules from the item being smelled get pulled into our nostrils when we take an inward breath. These molecules trigger olfactory sensors inside the nostrils. These sensors send electric signals to the brain; the brain then announces what it perceives us smelling.

Chapter Forty-Three
Take It with a Grain of Salt

Meaning

To not fully trust what one is reading or being told.

How It Came to Be

Salt is one of the most versatile products on earth. Researchers have listed over 14,000 uses for salt. You likely know it can be placed on food to help bring out the taste, but did you also know that it can be used as a(n)

- Insecticide; place it on your window sill to discourage ants.
- Weedkiller; sprinkle it on the grass in cracks on the sidewalk, and the grass will die.
- Ice melter; highway crews sprinkle it on roads to melt winter ice.
- Lubricant; put salt on the griddle, and the pancakes won't stick.

One thing salt was credited with doing in the Roman Empire that it may not have done was to serve as an antidote to poison. Based on documents written around 77 A.D. by Pliny the Elder, *Naturalis Historia*, if poison and salt were consumed simultaneously, any effects of the poison were thought to be neutralized. Some Roman leaders would deliberately consume small doses of poison to build up an intolerance to the poison, and they were taking the salt to make the poison more palatable. Whether kept for emergencies or pinched daily, salt became associated with neutralizing poison.

Advertisers, politicians, and even our friends often tell us things that may or may not be true. The ideas they are sharing can pollute our thinking if we accept them without carefully looking at them. Therefore, when we are presented with such an idea, we will "take it with a grain of salt;" we will listen to what they say but be very skeptical. The Roman leaders took their suspicious drinks with salt. Likewise, good readers look at new ideas skeptically, realizing the author may be inaccurate, have misleading information, or have left out a key detail.

FUN FACTS

chapter 43

- The saying, "Take it with a grain of salt," is the Americanized version of the saying; in England, it is rephrased as "Take it with a pinch of salt."
- A "grain of salt" weighs 65 mg.
- Salt and gold used to be traded ounce per ounce.
- Because of salt's ability to preserve food, many early human settlements were located where water and salt could be found.
- People need 200 milligrams of salt daily to be healthy; too much salt can lead to the body retaining too much water.

Chapter Forty-Four
Takes the Cake

Meaning

To be the very best (or the very worst, depending on one's point of view).

How It Came to Be

If there is an essay contest, decorating contest, bake-off contest, and any other similar competition in your community, what do people offer as prizes? The prize is often money in my town, but it has also been gift cards, a book, a candy bar, and a t-shirt. In many cases, it's not the prize that brings happiness but the thrill of winning something.

In ancient Greece, the prize for winning a contest was often a cake. For instance, if a person stayed up all night at many social gatherings, that person received a cake. "Taking the cake" meant being the best or the most foolish; not everybody thought staying up all night was a good idea. Today, "taking the cake" still means the same thing, to be out of the ordinary –whether that is a good thing or a bad thing depends on one's point of view.

In the 1800s, a game was invented that was built around this idiom. Schools, churches, and other community social groups would sponsor a carnival and include a cakewalk as one of the games. A representative cakewalk would look like this: Numbers 1-25 would be laid out in a circle, and participants would pay to stand on a number. Once every number had a person, the people would walk as music played; when the host stopped the music, everyone stopped at the number they were at. The host would then reach inside a hat, draw out a number, and that person would receive a cake that had been donated to be used as a prize. Those who did not know that the idiom "takes the cake" returned to ancient Greece and naturally associated the idiom with the cakewalk.

Now, you may think that The Cakewalk game is the source of the idiom "cakewalk," meaning that something is easy, but that is not where that idiom comes from. The "Cakewalk" was a dance performed by African Americans in the 1800s; its moves were easy to learn. From that dance, we get the idiom, "It was a cakewalk," something we say when we want to express that something is easy. Now, doesn't that take the cake?

FUN FACTS

chapter 44

- Many cakes consist of three layers - a layer of cake, a layer of frosting, and another layer of cake. This middle layer is called "the whoopie pie."
- The Egyptians created the first cake – it consisted of milk, honey, and flour - over six thousand years ago.
- Another idiom featuring cake is "a piece of cake," an idiom meaning "easy."

Chapter Forty-Five
Talk Turkey

Meaning

To talk frankly.

How It Came to Be

There is little doubt that the turkey is named with the country Turkey and its citizens in mind. However, it may not have anything to do with Turkey in particular. The British colonists – all Americans were British in those days -who first saw the bird were impressed with it. It was strange and exotic; anything strange and exotic was called

Turkish. On the other hand, the British marketplace did contain large game birds from Turkey, so it is possible the colonists had the country in mind.

Regardless, the British called the big game bird a turkey, and it is from that big game bird that we get the phrase "talk turkey." The phrase did not appear in print until 1824, but it was likely to be widely used in the colonial era. No one knows who first said it, but it is attributed to a Native American, sometimes identified as Wampum. The Native American and a pilgrim had spent the day gathering food and were dividing the finds at the end of the day. The pilgrim thought he'd be sly and asked, "What do you want me to do? Do you want me to take the turkey, and you take the crow, or do you want to take the crow, and I'll take the turkey?" The Native American listened to the two offers and replied, "You no talk turkey with me." "Talking turkey," in this case, was meant literally and figuratively, as in "you are not talking frank and honest with me." Since the pilgrims and the Native Americans often bargained for turkeys, the phrase, "You come to talk turkey?" became a greeting.

Eventually, talking turkey took on the opposite meaning. People who talked turkey sat around and joked. Talking turkey was lighthearted banter. This frivolity led to movies that were duds in the 1920s being called "turkeys." In the 1950s, children teased each other by calling one another a "turkey."

Today, the idiom is in the process of returning to its original meaning of talking frankly. Let's talk turkey for a minute - this idiom may be misunderstood, so if you use it, be sure your audience will interpret it as you intend.

FUN FACTS

chapter 45

- Male turkeys can be distinguished from female turkeys by the colors of their feathers. Male turkeys have bronze, brown, copper, gold, green, red, and purple feathers. Female turkeys have brown and gray feathers.
- A male turkey is a "gobbler," and a female turkey is a "hen."
- Wild turkeys can fly up to 55 miles per hour but can't fly long distances.
- That gobbling sound you hear are male turkeys. Female turkeys don't gobble.
- In bowling, "a turkey" is three consecutive strikes. The term originated because bowling alleys used the turkey as a marketing gimmick to attract people to the bowling alley; the bowling alley management would give a frozen turkey to anyone who threw three consecutive strikes.

Chapter Forty-Six
Talk Until I'm Blue in the Face

Meaning

To have talked passionately for a long time but seemingly accomplished nothing.

How It Came to Be

Breathe in.
Breathe out.

Until someone or something obstructs our airways, breathing in and out is an unconscious act that our body does about twenty to thirty times per minute. In each breath we take in, we provide our bodies with oxygen. The inhaled oxygen goes into our lungs and, from there, is dispersed to every cell and tissue in our body.

If your body does not get enough oxygen, you may notice that your heart is beating fast, that you seem dizzy and confused, that you have headaches, and – what's important for us when looking at this idiom – is that your skin may turn colors. People with a severe lack of oxygen will have blue skin.

If your mom or dad ever lectured until they were blue in the face, they were blue because they did not stop talking long enough to breathe properly, and their body was craving oxygen. Although people can talk until they are literally blue in the face, most people use the term figuratively; they do not endanger their health.

The idiom "feeling blue" is based on the same principle. In many cases, people who are very sick are not getting enough oxygen, and the reverse is also true;

people who are not getting enough oxygen are very sick. Medical science of the early 1800s may not have known a lot compared to what we know today. Still, people did recognize that if the body turned blue, something was wrong, and "feeling blue" began as a physical phenomenon and moved into mental health as well.

Even the concept of "having the blues" references being sick. Blues musicians have expanded their material from physical illness to include their soulmate leaving them, being alone in a city, and even having their dog abandon them.

Although people often say they will "talk until I'm blue in the face," the idiom "until I'm blue in the face" can accompany any activity, not just talking. For instance, you could "do homework until I'm blue in the face" or "eat pizza until I'm blue in the face." People who will do something until they are "blue in the face" are passionate about what they do and plan to continue doing it even if the odds of success are low.

FUN FACTS
chapter 46

- The muscle that helps the lungs to breathe is "the diaphragm."
- An active person will breathe in and out more than 50,000 times daily.
- "Don't waste your breath" is another idiom that one's talk will not influence another person.

Chapter Forty-Seven
Turn a Blind Eye

Meaning

To ignore something that one does not want to deal with.

How It Came to Be

As a youth, did you ever pretend that you were a pirate? If you did, you likely made an eyepatch from paper and string. Have you ever wondered why pirates wore eye patches? The reason for eye patches varied. Some pirates wore them to hide their identity; they might have known people on the boats they raided. Other pirates wore them to hide a disfiguration; some had lost an eye in battle. Others wore the patch to get their eyes used to a dark environment, allowing them to adjust to low lighting much faster than their enemies.

Go ahead and cover one of your eyes. Now, using your exposed eye, write what you see. Next, close your exposed eye and use your covered eye to write what you see.

You likely saw quite a bit of detail with your exposed eye. You might have seen more side detail if the second eye had been available, but you saw quite a lot. However, if your eyepatch was thick, you likely saw nothing in the second case. In this latter case, your eye was wide open, but it could not see anything. When you turn a blind eye to something, you can look directly at it but see nothing.

Horatio Nelson had lost sight in an eye in a battle early in his career. He had overcome this disability and risen through the ranks to vice admiral; by 1801, he was captaining a boat in a fleet at the Battle of Copenhagen. During the April 2 battle, the fleet commander signaled – they used big flags to communicate – that Nelson should retreat. An officer supposedly handed Nelson the telescope so he could see the flag for himself as he told Nelson the news. Nelson held the telescope to his bad eye, said he didn't see a thing and kept fighting.

The commander had Nelson court marshaled for disobeying orders. However, because Nelson had snatched victory from defeat, he was hailed a hero by the court and was promoted to fleet commander. Nelson's public trial following this historical incident of "turning a blind eye" made the idiom "turning a blind eye" a commonplace way to express, "I'm pretending not to see something I clearly know is there."

People often turn a blind eye to not seeing a rule being broken. For instance, a teacher may see two people talking in class but won't stop the lesson. One can also turn a blind eye to one's circumstances, too. For instance, your room may have clothes littered that need hanging, but you turn a blind eye and pretend they are not there. In many cases, both the person with the blind eye and the person doing what should not be being done have an unspoken code of "if you don't ask, I don't tell;" both know the offense is happening, but both pretend that it is not.

FUN FACTS

chapter 47

- Using flags or paddles to communicate as the British boats did at the Battle of Copenhagen is called "flag semaphore;" semaphore is the Greek word for "sign bearer." The flags are placed in different positions, and each position has a meaning.
- Although Nelson's life may have originated and spread the idiom, "turn a blind eye," there was a much older – and similar – idiom about a blind eye: "to turn a deaf ear and a blind eye."
- The typical pirate eye patch was constructed of cloth or leather, and it was held on one's face with either string or a leather strap.

Chapter Forty-Eight
Under Wraps

Meaning

To keep it a secret.

How It Came to Be

Don't you love birthdays and gift-giving holidays? On special occasions, people will put a treasure in a box, wrap it, and then present it to you – unless they are a tad lazy, and then they will put it in a bag, place tissue paper on top, and then present it to you. My guess is that you look at the box, maybe even gently shake it, and try to figure out what is inside. When something is under wraps, it is a secret.

Although exchanging gifts perfectly describes how we use the idiom "under wraps," and people would likely accept this as the explanation if I offered it, I would be lying. The origin of the idiom "under wraps" has nothing to do with gift-giving. Instead, it has to do with horse racing!

For the past 200 years, horse racing has been a sport that gamblers like to engage in. Before the race, the odds of a horse winning are determined by the oddsmakers. The less likely a horse is to win, the bigger the payday if it does win. This means that if the horse that is expected to win succeeds in winning, the gambler collects a small payday. On the other hand, if a horse that no one thought had a chance to win is declared the winner, the gambler gets a lot more money. Therefore, it is in the gambler's best interest that a good horse has a reputation as a loser; the good horse's speed should be kept "under wraps."

Jockeys keep horses from running fast by pulling back on the reins; they wrap them around their hands. Hence, keeping a horse under wraps meant for the jockey to keep the horse from running at full speed.

The idiom "under wraps" may have come from the sport of horse racing in the 1890s, but it quickly became accepted in other sports and by the public. Gift-giving may not be the source of this idiom, but it is responsible for its wide use. Because almost everyone has participated in giving wrapped packages, the concept of under wraps is something to which almost everyone can relate.

FUN FACTS

chapter 48

- Each year, over $1 billion is bet on horses.
- The typical racehorse weighs 1,000 pounds – that's half a ton!
- The idiom "big-hearted" – meaning to be kind, generous, and willing to help- also has roots in horse racing; a horse with a big heart can run faster than one with a small heart.

Chapter Forty-Nine
Up in the Air

Meaning

Undecided.

How It Came to Be

Step outside for a minute and look up in the air. Do you see a speck in the distance on the blue tapestry of the sky?
Is that a bird?
A satellite? A planet? A star?
A commercial airplane?
A military jet? A helicopter?
A hot air balloon?
Something else? If all you can see is a speck, you can't say with certainty what it is; all you can say is that it is up in the air.

Anything that is "up in the air" is uncertain. Just as you can observe more details about that little speck as it moves closer to you, you can figuratively get a better understanding of the project or idea that is "up in the air" as you become more acquainted with it. When something is up in the air, you can say it certainly exists, but beyond that, you may not be able to commit too much.

The phrase "up in the air" emerged in the early 1900s when airplanes first took to the skies and bystanders on the ground would try to distinguish one type of plane from another. Although "up in the air" began as a literal expression referring to aircraft, it quickly became an idiom referring to uncertainty.

Although "up in the air" was a new idiom in the early 1900s, it sounded pleasant because people had been saying a related idiom, "in the air," since the mid-1700s. When "in the air" began, people began learning about bacteria and germs. Beginning in the 1700s, people realized the air was full of literal contaminators, things that could rarely be seen but were definitely there. "Up in the air" was applied to concepts as well as physical objects; for instance, people may refer to "tension" being in the air or "autumn" being in the air.

FUN FACTS

chapter 49

- Orville and Wilbur Wright flew the first airplane, the Wright Flyer, at Kitty Hawk, North Carolina, on December 17, 1903.
- People suspected bacteria existed decades before it was seen. No one saw bacteria until 1674 when Dutch scientist Antonie van Leeuwenhoek looked through the newly invented microscope and saw them in pond water and human mouth scrapings. He called the previously invisible creatures "animalcules."
- Bacteria is Earth's oldest life form.

Chapter Fifty
Zombie Apocalypse

Meaning

In a general sense, this term means "the worst catastrophe imaginable; an unexpected terrible event that will bring destruction and chaos;" in a specific sense, it means "Zombies bring about the end of the world as we know it."

How It Came to Be

It's the end of the world – or at least the end of this book.

Have you ever wondered how the world will end? Let me assure you, you are not alone in wondering.

Since some people ask how it will end, we should not be surprised that others have tried to answer that question. Both religion and science have addressed it. In our culture, the most famous religious answer is the "apocalypse" described in the Bible's book of Revelation. Believe it or not, "apocalypse" does not mean "the end of the world." "Apocalypse" is a Greek word that means "uncovering;" when John received his vision of the last days, he received a clue to the mystery. Up until the days of John, any clue to a mystery could have been an "apocalypse." Over time, though, thanks to John, a discussion of the end of time became known as "the apocalypse"; if one talked about John's vision in particular, it was "The Apocalypse." Today, "apocalypse" refers to the end of time or, in some less severe cases, the end of time as we know it.

Scientists, too, offer speculation about how the world will end. They believe that the sun will one day burn out. Most scientists think the end of the world – or at least the end of the human race - will happen long before that because of climate change, overpopulation, pollution, and nuclear war.

People try to prepare for the worst to ensure the human race survives. For instance, those who believe the threat of nuclear war in one's area is real will build underground bunkers and stock food. Survivalists try to imagine the most unimaginable phenomena and determine how to cope.

For the past several years, the possibility of people from the past coming back to life and feasting on today's people has been the greatest fear imaginable. People from the past who come back to life are called zombies in folklore. Haitian folklore has stories of how voodoo cults can bring the dead back to life. Once back to life, the zombies want to torment and even eat the living. The idiom suggests that one can survive anything if one is prepared for the Zombie Apocalypse, the worst of all possible apocalypses.

FUN FACTS

chapter 50

- Zombies did not become a well-known phenomenon until 1927. That year, *The Magic Island*, a book by W.B. Seabrook, introduced Western culture to the zombies found in Haitian folklore.
- The original zombies described in Haiti looked like ordinary people except for their eyes. They also acted like ordinary people, except they were emotionless.
- The U.S. military occupied Haiti in 1915, and soldiers heard zombie stories and shared these stories back in the United States. They added details, and the graphic novels and movies that shared them with the public embellished even more. Zombies became blood-thirsty and nearly indestructible.
- *Night of the Living Dead*, a horror film, came out in 1968, and from it spouted the mindset people have of zombies today, the ideas that fill video games, graphic movies, numerous graphic novels, and, of course, The Zombie Apocalypse.

Did You Enjoy The Book ?

If you did, we are ecstatic. If not, please write your complaint to us and we will ensure we fix it.

If you're feeling generous, there is something important that you can help me with – tell other people that you enjoyed the book.

Ask a grown-up to write about it on Amazon. When they do, more people will find out about the book. It also lets Amazon know that we are making kids around the world laugh. Even a few words and ratings would go a long way.

If you have any ideas or jokes that you think are super funny, please let us know. We would love to hear from you.

Our email address is -
riddleland@riddlelandforkids.com

Riddleland Bonus

Join our **Facebook Group** at **Riddleland for Kids**
to get daily jokes and riddles.

https://pixelfy.me/riddlelandbonus

Thank you for buying this book. As a token of our appreciation,
we would like to offer a special bonus—a collection of 50
original jokes, riddles, and funny stories.

Other Fun Books by Riddleland
Riddles Series

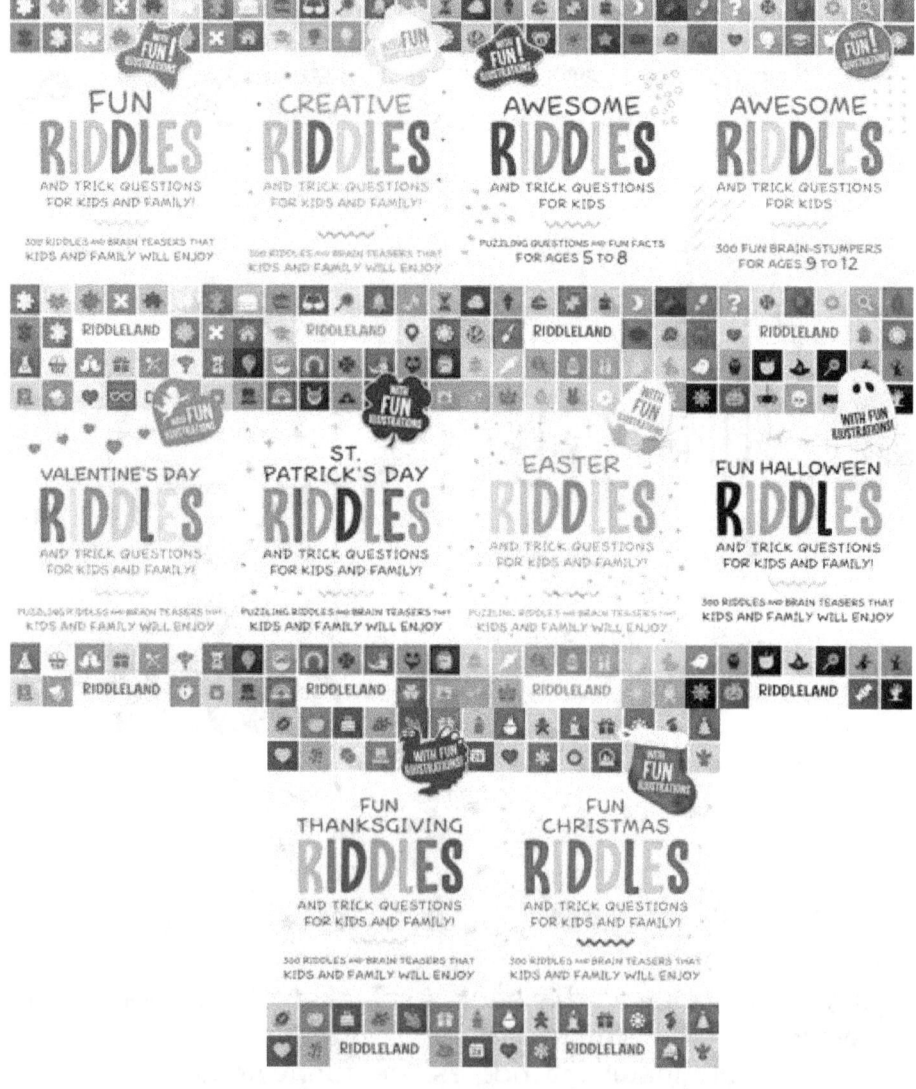

It's Laugh O'Clock Joke Books

Would You Rather...Series

Get them on Amazon or our website at
www.riddlelandforkids.com

About Riddleland

Riddleland is a mum + dad run publishing company. We are passionate about creating fun and innovative books to help children develop their reading skills and fall in love with reading. If you have suggestions for us or want to work with us, shoot us an email at

riddleland@riddlelandforkids.com

Our favourite family quote

"Creativity is an area in which younger people have a tremendous advantage since they have an endearing habit of always questioning past wisdom and authority."

— Bill Hewlett

www.ingramcontent.com/pod-product-compliance
Lightning Source LLC
Chambersburg PA
CBHW071020120626
46546CB00003B/1167